Helping Children Cope With Fears and Stress

Part I: Discussion and Activities
Part II: Facilitator's Guide

Edward H. Robinson
Joseph C. Rotter
Mary Ann Fey
Kenneth R. Vogel

ERIC Counseling and Personnel Services Clearinghouse
2108 School of Education
The University of Michigan
Ann Arbor, Michigan 48109-1259

Based on a publication developed by the Department of Educational Psychology at the University of South Carolina in Columbia and originally published through a grant from the Overseas Schools Advisory Council awarded to the Association of International Schools in Africa.

ERIC Counseling and Student Services Clearinghouse
School of Education
University of North Carolina at Greensboro
Greensboro, North Carolina 27412-5001

ISBN 1-56109-041-7

This publication was prepared with partial funding from the Office of Educational Research and Improvement, U.S. Department of Education under contract no. RI88062011. The opinions expressed in this report do not necessarily reflect the positions or policies of OERI, the Department of Education, or ERIC/CASS.

Contents

Part 2: Facilitator's Guide

List of Handouts

Preface

There are a number of things that excite me about *Helping Children Cope With Fears and Stress*. First, it clearly responds to a present and growing need for a resource book that will help counselors, teachers and educators to better understand how fears, phobias, anxiety and stress develop in children (K–8), and how they (children) can be assisted in successfully coping with omnipresent fears and stress. Second, in a highly gratifying and much needed departure from the usual practice of offering up generalized "cookbook" approaches, the authors have developed 47 specific activities. Each of the activities is designed to assist a child in coping with a particular aspect of fear or stress. Some are designed to assist children in coping with extant fears and stress, while others focus on fear prevention, stress reduction or helping high-risk students. A third attractive and most useful feature of this book is a facilitator's guide which will assist the counselor, teacher or educator to more effectively intervene with children and to make better use of the activities provided. Fourth, this is not a book filled with pipe dreams. The authors have validated the concepts and activities through extensive field testing with schools and students in this country and overseas.

My list of what I like about *Helping Children Cope With Fears and Stress* could go on endlessly. Suffice to say it is a book that is both practical and substantive and will be of inestimable use to counselors, teachers and educators.

Garry R. Walz
Director

About the Authors

Edward H. Robinson, Ph.D., is a professor in the Department of Educational Psychology at the University of South Carolina in Columbia.

Joseph C. Rotter, Ph.D., is a professor in and chairperson of the Department of Educational Psychology at the University of South Carolina in Columbia.

Mary Ann Fey, M.Ed., NCC, is an elementary school counselor at St. Joseph's Elementary School in Columbia, South Carolina.

Kenneth R. Vogel, MA, is headmaster at the International School of Ouagadougou in Burkina Faso, Africa.

How to Use This Book

Helping Children Cope With Fears and Stress is meant to be used by teachers, school counselors and school administrators.

Part 1: Discussion and Activities

Part 1: Discussion and Activities contains activities which complement the various curricular areas of a typical elementary school and which can be integrated into normal instruction without the disruption that a separate "Unit" on fears or stress would entail. To make the activities easier to use, each one includes the curricular areas into which it would fit (i.e., Language Arts, Social Studies, etc.), the grade levels and group size for which it is suitable, and the approximate time necessary for its completion. **Part 1** is divided into sections as follows:

Section 1 is an Introduction to the origin of fears and stress in children and to the theory which underlies our model of successful coping.

Section 2 deals with Fear Specific Activities; that is, activities which address themselves to the alleviation of the effects of fear and to specific fears, such as the fear of the dark or the first day of school.

Section 3 comprises general activities used for the Prevention of fear and to build up children's feelings of security, self-worth and control.

Section 4 introduces Stress Reducing Activities with a variety of scripts that can be used at various grade levels.

Section 5 includes activities to help allay the fears of non-English speaking students, and to help children express feelings and thoughts related to a personal or a collective crisis event and help them develop coping strategies.

Section 6 includes four Appendices: **Appendix 1-A** discusses high risk children in schools. **Appendix 1-B** presents a model of counseling which can be used with children who have suffered a trauma or who have not developed successful coping skills. **Appendix 1-C** is a Bibliography of children's books, arranged by fear, author and grade level which can be used by teachers or counselors for bibliotherapeutic purposes. **Appendix 1-D** is a list of other Resources which may be helpful to the educator interested in developing a collection of materials dealing with fears and stress.

Part 2: Facilitator's Guide

Part 2 is divided into eight sessions and three appendices. The purpose of this guide is to provide training to teachers and counselors who wish to learn how to help children cope with fears and stress.

Session 1 provides an opportunity for participants to briefly share something about themselves and establish an atmosphere of relaxed sharing as they begin to explore the typical fears and stress of children.

Session 2 addresses the three levels of primary prevention: developmental, high risk and treatment. An overview of the levels is presented followed by an indepth study of the first level of prevention (developmental) and related intervention strategies.

Session 3 provides teachers and school counselors with ideas for activities they can do with children to help them develop the knowledge and skills necessary for coping with fears and stress.

Session 4 helps teachers and school counselors recognize potential high risk children and develop the knowledge and skills necessary for helping these children.

Session 5 helps teachers and school counselors develop an understanding of how to help children cope with their fears and stress during either a collective or an individual crisis.

Session 6 helps teachers and school counselors develop an understanding of how to help children who are not coping well in their lives because of the effect of fears and stress, and help identify potential resources and strategies for helping these children.

Session 7 focuses on fear and stress as family issues. Although fear and stress may be triggered by isolated incidences, their effect on children often results from the amount of advanced preparation parents have made and their ability to effectively follow up on stressful situations.

Session 8 emphasizes the three levels of prevention with a focus on infusion of activities on fear and stress into the daily curriculum. This final session is the most important part of the training, for it is through the plan of action developed by the teachers and counselors that the program will or will not reach success.

Appendix 2-A is a Fear and Stress Survey, **Appendix 2-B** consists of Handouts, and **Appendix 2-C** is Activities for Children Exposed to a Violent Event.

We recommend that *Helping Children Cope With Fears and Stress* be placed in the school's professional collection for easy access and that the activities in Part 1 be removed and duplicated by counselors and teachers for use in their classrooms.

Part 1

Discussion and Activities

Section 1

Overview of Fears and Stress in Children

Overview of Fears and Stress in Children

Introduction

Childhood is generally a positive time of life filled with promise, hope and wonder. It can also be a time of stress and fear as the demands of a rapidly changing world and the rising expectations of modern life take their toll. Although learning to deal with stressors is a normal part of growing up, many children develop inadequate or inappropriate coping strategies. Researchers have linked this inability to cope appropriately to the increasing rate of teen and pre-teen suicide, substance abuse, teen pregnancy and academic failure. Since the consequences of fears and stress can be so serious, it behooves us as educators to be cognizant of the signs of fears and stress among our students and to be aware of activities and strategies that may help to alleviate or prevent their deleterious effects.

The purpose of this publication, then, is to offer to teachers a brief introduction to the topic of children's fears and stress and a guide to activities and strategies which can be integrated into the curriculum from kindergarten through grade eight. These activities are meant to be useful for purposes of prevention, and, in some cases, remediation of the effects of fears and stress. In addition, they are structured so as to fit within the typical elementary school or middle school curriculum rather than treated as one more "subject" added to an already over-crowded school day.

As part of the introduction to the guide, definitions of the various types of fears will be presented and the results of recent investigations into the nature of fears in children will be discussed.

Fears, Phobias, Anxiety and Stress

Fear can be defined as an affective (feeling), cognitive (thinking), motoric (behaving) and physiological (bodily changes) response to a perceived threat. It is generally a response to a specific object or concept, such as a snake or being left alone. Fear is a normal part of the developing process and can be an important tool for self-preservation. Faced with a fear object, such as an oncoming truck, a child's fear response (distress, recognition of real danger, increased heart rate and adrenaline, and fleeing) is quite appropriate and even necessary for the continued existence of the organism.

Phobias are a type of fear which is largely irrational and out of proportion to the threat. The focus of a phobia is usually specific, such as the fear of flying or of heights, yet the source is not necessarily immediately threatening to the victim. Phobias in children are often associated with school.

Anxiety is a feeling of uneasiness or doom whose source is uncertain and vague. The person suffering from anxiety may not be able to pinpoint the cause nor even specify the nature of the doom which the anxiety portends. Nevertheless, the effects of anxiety can be just as debilitating as if the source were real and specific.

Stress can be defined as tension caused by a positive or negative event. It can serve as a warning signal or can lead to problems such as tension headaches, ulcers and other physiological and psychological impairments. Deadlines and overwork, lack of sleep, rapid changes, familial and environmental crises, and culture shock are examples of sources of stress in both children and adults.

The fear cycle in children is illustrated in the following figure.

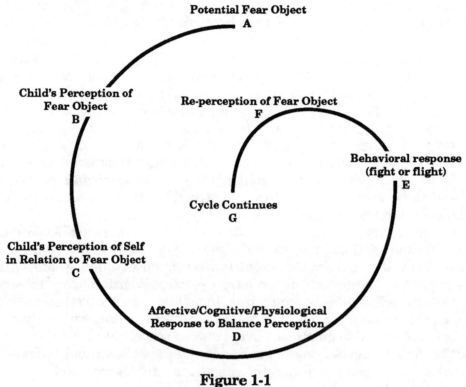

Figure 1-1
Conceptualization of the Fear Cycle

Learning to cope with fears is a part of the normal process of child development. It is when children develop inappropriate responses or inadequate coping strategies that fears become a problem. Studies have shown that one in five children suffer from debilitating forms of test anxiety that inhibit their school performance (Deffenbacher, Michaels, Michaels, & Daley, 1986; Deffenbacher & Michaels, 1981; Phillips, 1978). One in ten children will develop phobic reactions to objects that most individuals will handle with ease (Robinson, Robinson, Whetsell, & Weber, 1986), and as mentioned earlier, increased stress in children's lives has been linked to other more severe consequences.

Sources of Fear in Children

Stress may affect the children's performance in school and result in behavioral and academic deficiencies which can be detected by the classroom teacher. The top fifteen children's fears cited by one group of teachers included the following:

Typical Fears of Children as Perceived by Teachers

1. Change of school
2. Failure at school
3. Being alone
4. Family strife
5. Punishment
6. Death
7. Darkness
8. Homework
9. Strangers
10. Monsters
11. Ghosts
12. Loss
13. Not being accepted
14. Nuclear war
15. Thieves

An international study of children's fears (Robinson, Robinson, Whetsell & Weber, 1986) surveyed the fears of children between the ages of four and fourteen and included subjects from the United States, South America, Africa and the Middle East. Through the use of a structured interview, the following fear objects were cited most often by the children:

Fears of Children Aged 4–14 in Six Countries as Perceived by Children

1. Darkness
2. Ghosts
3. Isolation
4. Nightmares
5. Punishment
6. Monsters
7. Other people in general
8. Specific people (robbers, etc.)
9. Being lost
10. Teachers

However, children from different cultures do not necessarily fear the same objects nor do they cite them in the same order. Different environments can contribute to different perceptions of what should and should not be frightening. For example, city children who are not exposed to natural phenomena would be less likely to cite particular animals as being fear provoking than rural children. Conversely, traffic would not be a great source of fear in rural settings. A comparison of the top ten fears of children from the U.S.A., Ecuador and Liberia demonstrates this difference rather clearly.

Fears of Children in Three Countries as Perceived by Children Aged 4–14

U.S.A.	Ecuador	Liberia
Darkness	Teachers	Ghosts
Ghosts	People	Nightmares
Robbers	Robbers	Monsters
Monsters	Animals	Snakes
Kidnappers	Darkness	Weapons
Isolation	Forgetting	Dogs
People	Insects	Santa Claus
Punishment	Isolation	Lions
Being lost	Strange noises	Insects
Strange noises	Illness	Cars

Table 1-1 on page 8 summarizes normative data on the chronological appearance of children's fears taken from a number of studies.

Table 1-1
Normative Data on Children's Fears

Age	Fears
0–6 months	Loss of support, loud noises, sudden movement
7–12 months	Strangers, sudden appearance of large objects, loud noises
1 year	Separation from parent, strangers, injury, toilet
2 years	large animals, dark rooms, large objects and machines, loud noises, sudden changes in personal environment
3 years	Dark rooms, masks, large animals, snakes, separation from parent
4 years	Dark rooms, noise at night, large animals, snakes, separation from parent
5 years	Wild animals, bodily injury, dark, bad people, separation from parent
6 years	Ghosts, monsters, witches, dark, storms, being alone, thunder and lightning
7 years	Dark, monsters, storms, being lost, kidnapping, being alone
8 years	Dark, people (kidnapper, robber, mugger), guns/weapons, being alone, animals
9 years	Dark, lost, bad dreams, bodily harm/accident, being alone
10 years	Dark, people, bad dreams, punishment, strangers
11 years	Dark, being alone, bad dreams, being hurt by someone, being sick, tests, grades
12 years	Dark, punishment (being in trouble, bad grades), being alone, being hurt or taken away, tests, grades
13 years	Crime in general, being hurt or kidnapped, being alone, war in general and nuclear war, bad grades, tests, punishment
14 years+	Failure at school, personal relations, war, tests, sex issues (pregnancy, AIDS), being alone, family concerns

Source: Croak & Know, 1971; Ilg & Ames, 1955; Jersild & Holmes, 1935; Kellerman, 1981; Maurer, 1965; Morris & Krotochwell, 1983; Robinson, Robinson, & Whetsell, 1988.

Fear objects apparently change with age and maturation. The fear of large animals is common in younger school-age children, but diminishes in older elementary-age children. Fear of death is not prevalent in the early years, but begins to be a concern for children in the elementary grades. Imaginary fear objects, such as monsters, ghosts and witches, diminish in middle school-age children and are replaced with, among other things, fears of nuclear war, muggers and failure in school. The fears of adolescence seem to revolve around personal and sexual identity, social acceptance, purpose in life and failure. Beginning in middle school and increasing through the high school years, representation of fear objects tends to become more vague. Thus, anxiety, rather than fear, may be a more useful term for a young person's reaction in the later school years (Rotter & Robinson, 1987).

The Foundations for Successful Coping

Children who have confidence in their ability to master and control events and challenges in their lives are less vulnerable to fear. These children have a sense of personal power. In contrast, a child who feels helpless in the face of danger is vulnerable to fears.

Children's perception of their power will influence their decision to fight to overcome the fear object or try to escape the fear object through flight. Children's sense of power in relationship to their environment and their ability to accurately assess the power of the fear object is central to learning to cope with fear. A realistic or unrealistic assessment of one's personal power with regard to a fear object can mean the difference between successful coping behaviors or a feeling of helplessness.

Power can be seen not only as an internal force, but also as external—the allies that the child has to bring to bear on the fear object. These allies can be parents, teachers, peers or anyone with whom the child has built a supportive relationship.

Related to power are three important constructs: self-worth, security and control. These concepts are explained in more detail below.

Self-Worth

Children who feel good about themselves, hold themselves in high esteem, and experience success in meeting normal developmental tasks have well developed concepts of self-worth. Based on this success identity, they are more likely to have the confidence needed to explore and attempt new strategies to overcome fears. A child with a positive sense of self-worth will perceive a move to a new school as an opportunity to meet new friends and experience new challenges.

Security

Children who have adults in their lives who care for and encourage them develop a sense of security. Because they have allies on whom they can count, they are able to build supportive interpersonal relationships with peers and adults. Children who are secure have little difficulty reaching out to others when faced with new situations and changes in their lives.

Control

Children who have been given some autonomy in decision making learn they have a degree of control over their lives. They learn to assess their strengths and weaknesses and accept that coping with dilemmas in life is a natural part of growing up. Faced with a potentially daunting situation, such as shopping in an open air market, children with a sense of control enter with confidence that they can succeed in mastering a new environment.

Implications for the Educator

This concept of the relationship between personal power in the face of one's normal fears and one's estimate of self-worth, security and control has important implications for the educator in helping children cope with normal fears as well as helping children whose over-reaction to fear is self-defeating and impeding normal growth and development. An understanding teacher can make a significant difference in the ability of children to cope with normal fears or a specific crisis evoking a fear response. It is important, then, that the teacher first be aware of those common fears that children experience at each stage of development.

Signs of Fear and Stress

The signs or symptoms of stress that children manifest are clues to teachers about the children's ability to cope with a specific fear or general anxiety. Some of these signs are obvious while others are covert and require some investigation. As educators, we should be aware of the signs of fear and stress in our students, preferably before the crisis stage is reached. As in most things, prevention is more sensible than remediation.

As a part of this project, a group of school teachers were asked to identify the outward signs of fears and stress in their students. The respondents generated an enormous number of signs which can be categorized into eight groups. Following is a summary of these findings:

Physical manifestations: Illnesses (real or imagined), head and stomach aches, frequent urination, tiredness, loss of weight, aches and pains, profuse sweating.

Emotional reactions: Crying, sensitivity, stammering, "hair trigger" responses, irritability, excess giggling, easily startled, sudden changes of expression, general unrest.

Work habits: Poor presentation of work, doodling, daydreaming, frequent absence, disorganization, cheating, sleeping in class, not staying on task, lack of concentration.

Nervous manifestations: Ticks, nail biting, blinking, hair chewing, sucking fingers, fidgeting, rocking motions, chewing clothing.

Misbehavior and aggression: Violence, breaking pencils, loss of temper, striking out, bad language, violent drawings, quarreling, uncontrollable rage, bullying, destructiveness, theft.

Attention seeking: Immature behavior, seeking approval, demands for attention, making up bizarre stories, continuous questioning, clinging to teacher, acting out, faking injuries.

Self-destructive tendencies: Suicide threats, suicide attempts, not caring what happens, self- denigration, alcohol and/or drug abuse.

The Role of the Teacher and Counselor

Children who are preoccupied with the stressors or fears they are attempting to cope with are not fully engaged in learning. Therefore, the role of the teacher is to find ways to integrate activities and resources into the classroom that will help all children cope with fears and stress. A developmental approach is the optimal way of helping children develop coping behaviors to interact with fears and stressors of their environment in a positive way so as to enhance growth. A developmental approach considers the nature of child development, the tasks to be accomplished, and the skills needed for continued growth.

Assessing the school environment to identify sources of fears and stress that can be eliminated or modified is an important place to begin. Then activities can be incorporated into the curriculum which enhance students' feelings of self-worth, security and control.

For example, activities which help students learn more about their own interests and personal strengths can enhance self-confidence and feelings of self-worth. Security can be increased with activities which facilitate the development of communication skills and positive interpersonal relationships with peers and adults. Problem solving skills and strategies that enhance decision making can increase children's sense of control in coping with the normal demands of fears and stressors in their environment.

Coping Through Self-Expression

Specific opportunities to explore and express the fears of childhood in a supportive setting help the child learn to cope. Expression itself can provide a release for much of the tensions brought on by stress and fear. Children are often reluctant to admit to fears because our culture teaches them that they are supposed to be brave. This "fear of admitting fear" can be overcome through capitalizing on the teachable moments as they arise and providing many varied opportunities and activities for children to express their fears openly and in a nonjudgmental atmosphere. In addition, being aware of unspoken fears and giving children the opportunity to reveal their concerns may reduce the potential for a traumatic experience and avoid the development of more intense fear.

Sometimes the immediacy of a crisis incident or the over-reaction of a particular child to a specific fear requires direct intervention. A fear may be disabling to the point of impeding the normal growth and development of the child. As a professional in the school setting, listening may be the most valuable service one can perform. Allowing students to unlock their feelings and articulate their fears is the beginning of helping children assess their own levels of security, control and self-worth.

Working in concert with the child's family and eliciting the support of other school professionals are further ways of offering direct help to the child. The teacher is often in the best position to notice aberrant behavior on the part of the child which may signal the need for intervention. Teachers can then make the proper referral to the school counselor, if one is available.

If no counseling professionals are on staff at the school, it would behoove teachers and the school administration to make an assessment of the mental health facilities within the community. Being familiar with the resources of the local community can be of vital importance in assisting the child and the family.

References

Deffenbacher, J. L., & Michaels, A. C. (1981). Anxiety management training and self control desensitization—15 months later. *Journal of Counseling Psychology, 28,* 459–462.

Deffenbacher, J. L., Michaels, A. C., Daley, P. C., & Michaels, T. (1980). Comparison of anxiety management training and self control desensitization. *Journal of Counseling Psychology, 27,* 232–239.

Phillips, B. N. (1978). *School stress and anxiety: Theory, research and intervention.* New York: Human Sciences Press.

Robinson, E. H., Robinson, S. L, Whetsell, M. V., & Weber, A. (1986, April). *Fear: A developmental perspective.* Presentation at the annual meeting of the American Association for Counseling and Development, Los Angeles.

Rotter, J. C., & Robinson, E. H. (1987). Coping with fear and stress: Classroom interventions. *International Quarterly, 5*(4), 39–44.

Section 2

Fear Specific Activities

Shadows

Fear:	The Dark
Curricular Areas:	Art, Science, Language Arts
Grades:	K–2
Size:	Full class
Time:	60–90 minutes
Purpose:	To help children cope with the fear of the dark by exploring the physical nature of shadows, the fears they feel, and how they can cope with those nighttime fears.

Outcomes:

The students will be able to:
1. explain the physical origin of shadows;
2. generate descriptive words about shadows;
3. create their own drawings or paintings of shadows;
4. identify ways of coping with shadow-related fears.

Materials:

1. Overhead or filmstrip projector (or flashlight)
2. Screen (or blank wall)
3. Large sheet of paper (or chalkboard)
4. White drawing paper
5. Black crayons or black paint and brushes

Procedures:

1. Using an overhead or filmstrip projector, have the children create shadows with their fingers and other objects, projecting them on a screen or wall, and discuss how shadows are made.
2. As a group activity, write on a large sheet of paper (or chalkboard) the words children use to describe the shadows and how they feel when they see shadows at night.
3. Provide materials for the children to draw or paint a shadow on a piece of white drawing paper.
4. As a group, encourage individuals to talk about their shadow pictures. Ask them what they do at night when they see shadows. Discuss with them what they might do the next time they see a shadow at night.

Coping strategy suggestions:
a. Turn a light on to make the shadow go away.
b. Tell yourself its only a shadow.
c. Get reassurance from a sibling or parent.
d. Turn on light to make your own shadows.

Puppets: Ghosts, Goblins and Monsters

Fear:	Imaginary Creatures
Curricular Areas:	Art, Music, Language Arts
Grades:	K–2
Size:	Full class
Time:	30 minutes
Purpose:	To help children cope with the fear of imaginary creatures by transforming their own versions of nightmares or monsters into paper string puppets.

Outcomes:

The students will be able to:
1. Create their own puppet version of an imaginary creature;
2. Share their nightmares with other students through puppetry;
3. Identify what the children in the story or song do to cope with their fears;
4. Discuss what they can do when they have a nightmare or feel threatened by frightening creatures in the dark.

Materials:

1. Book: *There's a Nightmare in My Closet* by Mercer Mayer or Song: "It Was All a Dream" on the album *Tickly Toddle* by Hap Palmer
2. Construction paper
3. Glue
4. String
5. Cardboard tube

Procedures:

1. Read the story to the class or play and sing the song and discuss the coping behaviors of the characters.
2. Give the students an opportunity to share their experiences with nightmares or imaginary creatures.
3. Provide them with materials and instructions to make their own paper string puppet versions of nightmares or monsters.
4. Allow children to interact with each other. Encourage them to provide voices for their puppets.
5. As closure to the activity, discuss with the children what they can do when they have nightmares or when they think there is a monster in the room.

Coping strategy suggestions:
a. Get reassurance from a parent or a sibling.
b. Turn on the light and examine the room.
c. Surround themselves with their own stuffed animals and playthings.
d. For nightmares, get a drink of water and reassure themselves that it was only a dream.

Fantasy Trip

Fears:	Strangers, New Places
Curricular Areas:	Science, Art, Social Studies, Language Arts
Grades:	K–2
Size:	Full class
Time:	180 minutes (several classes)
Purpose:	To help children explore feelings associated with unfamiliar people and places and to realize what we can do to make unfamiliar things more familiar.

Outcomes: *The students will be able to:*
1. Identify situations and people that may be strange or unfamiliar;
2. Create an imaginary world;
3. Identify familiar and unfamiliar people and things on the school campus;
4. Discuss the people and things that were strange and are now familiar and comfortable.

Materials:
1. Book: *Where the Wild Things Are* by Maurice Sendak.
2. Clay
3. Boxes
4. Paper
5. Paint
6. Portable tape recorder
7. Blank audio tape

Procedures:
1. Introduce and read the book, *Where the Wild Things Are*. Discuss Max's trip to an imaginary world and the strange creatures he found there.
2. Expand the discussion by asking the students to talk about:
   a. if they'd like to travel in space;
   b. if they wonder what other worlds and the people who live there might be like;
   c. what it would be like to be a tiny bug or giant in the world;
   d. what it would be like to be on the bottom of the ocean and what kinds of life would be found there.
3. Have the children make a model of an imaginary world. They could use clay, boxes, paper and paint to create a world different from ours. They could describe people and animals that live there—what they eat, where and how they live, and so on. Allow time to share and discuss their world.
4. Take a walk around the school campus. Look for familiar and unfamiliar people, places and things. When an unfamiliar person, place or thing is encountered, examine, explain or introduce the students to the unfamiliar thing in order to familiarize them with it. Tape record what the children think and feel about what they see. Listen to the recording in the classroom and discuss how unfamiliar things become familiar.

Using Children's Literature

Fear:	Any Fear
Curricular Area:	Language Arts
Grades:	K–2
Size:	Full class
Time:	30 minutes
Purpose:	To help children realize that others share the same fears and to help them cope with their fears.

Outcomes:

The students will be able to:
1. Identify the character's fear after listening to the story;
2. Discuss their own experiences with this fear;
3. Identify ways the character coped with his/her fear;
4. Generate ways of coping with this fear the next time it is encountered.

Materials:

A story selected from the *Bibliography of Children's Fears* (see Appendix C) or another story which addresses a childhood fear and in which the character(s) is able to cope with his/her fear.

Procedures:

1. Introduce the story and read it to the children. Ask them to listen for what the character(s) is afraid of and what the character(s) does when he/she is afraid.
2. Discuss the story with the children. Ask the children to talk about:
   a. the character and what the character was afraid of;
   b. times they have experienced a similar fear;
   c. how they felt inside when they were afraid;
   d. what the character did in the story to cope with his/her fear;
   e. what they do to help themselves when they are afraid;
   f. what they might do the next time they experience this fear.

Discussion of the story is the crucial part of this activity. It provides opportunities for students to share how they would feel, think and act in a similar situation and learn how the story character or other peers would cope with the same situation.

Moving

Fear:	Moving
Curricular Areas:	Language Arts, Math, Art, Social Studies
Grades:	3–5
Size:	Full class
Time:	120 minutes (several classes)
Purpose:	To help children express and share the common anxieties and stressors that may accompany moving to a new home.

Outcomes:

The students will be able to:
1. Identify and discuss the stressors and anxieties experienced by families in moving;
2. Create a mural showing the sequence of events in moving from one home to another;
3. Build models of different kinds of houses used around the world;
4. Use maps to calculate distances between places.

Materials:

1. Mural paper
2. Crayons, paint or markers
3. Materials for building house models, such as clay, straws, wooden sticks, sugar cubes, cardboard, glue, etc.

Procedures:

1. Discuss with the children:
   a. reasons why families move;
   b. how a family gets ready for a move;
   c. problems a family faces when they move;
   d. various ways furniture and belongings are moved from one place to another;
   e. the students' experiences with moving;
   f. how it feels to be in a new neighborhood without any friends;
   g. what you can do to make friends in a new place;
   h. how you can help a new child who moves into your area.
2. Students can break up into small groups to work on one of the following activities or the activity's length can be extended so that every student can experience doing each activity.
   a. *Murals:* Create a mural showing the sequence of events in moving from one home to another (i.e., garage sales, packing, traveling, etc.). Dialogue can be added to the characters shown.
   b. *Models:* Build models of different kinds of houses used around the world, such as apartment buildings, frame houses, igloos, mud huts, straw houses, stone houses, etc. Have the children create backdrops behind the models, showing the countryside that would be found around the dwellings.

c. *Map Math:* Have the students calculate the distances between cities and countries around the world. Have students figure out whose hometown is farthest away from the school and whose hometown is the closest.
d. *Hometown Sharing:* Have students give reports on their hometowns, comparing and contrasting them with where they are living now.
e. Be sure to take time to share and discuss projects.

The Worry Game

Fear:	New School
Curricular Area:	Social Studies
Grades:	3–5
Size:	Full class
Time:	30 minutes
Purpose:	To help children realize that other students share anxieties about being in a new school setting and help them cope with those fears.
Outcomes:	*The students will be able to:*

The students will be able to:
1. Identify some worries associated with being in a new school setting;
2. Make decisions about coping strategies to deal with new school settings.

Materials: None

Procedures:

1. Divide the group into two teams, the Worriers and the Doers. The task of the Worrier team is to suggest things that might go wrong, be scary or cause worry on the first day of school. The task of the Doer team is to suggest solutions to the problems posed by the Worrier team members. If the problem is something for which there is no solution, then the Doers must suggest how a student could make the best of it.
2. Begin the game with the sentence: *"Tomorrow is your first day in a new school."*
3. Have the first Worrier team member make a suggestion of what might go wrong, be scary or cause worry. Collaboration is encouraged.
4. Have the first Doer team member provide a suggestion or decision to overcome the worry. Collaboration is encouraged.
5. If the Doer can make a reasonable suggestion (the teacher can be the judge), then the Doer team gets a point. If not, then the Worrier team gets a point. Continue on until all team members have had a chance to articulate a concern or a solution.
6. If time permits, have the teams switch roles. The team with the most points wins.

Writing About Fears

Fear:	Any Fear
Curricular Area:	Language Arts
Grades:	3–5
Size:	Full class
Time:	60 minutes
Purpose:	To help children express and share their fears and coping strategies through writing.
Outcome:	*The students will be able to:*

Outcome:

The students will be able to:
1. Create stories and poetry about fears;
2. Share their stories with their peers;
3. Identify alternate modes of coping with their fears.

Materials:
1. Composition paper
2. Pencil or pen

Procedures:

Activity One: Story Starters

Give the students one or all of the following topic sentences to begin short stories:
1. "Everybody is afraid sometimes. I remember when..."
2. "The scariest place I've ever been was..."
3. "I am a furry monster hiding in a child's dark closet. I feel..."

Activity Two: Story Building

1. Students choose an object or noun and make up a group story about it. The following sequence is an example that could easily lead to a story about haunted houses:
   a. Student 1: "I see a house."
   b. Student 2: "The house is red."
   c. Student 3: "The red house is spooky."
   d. Student 4: "The spooky red house has spiderwebs in the window."
2. Students can continue with their own story.

Activity Three: Cinquains

1. A cinquain is a five line poem with a 2 syllable word on the first and last lines and 4, 6 and 8 syllables on the second, third and fourth lines. An example follows:

Nighttime	2 syllables
Monsters, scary	4 syllables
Hiding, jumping, laughing	6 syllables
Come out in my bedroom at night	8 syllables
Daytime	2 syllables

After each of these writing activities, allow time to share the stories or poetry and discuss alternate means of coping with the fears expressed in the writing.

Using Children's Literature

Fear:	Any Fear
Curricular Area:	Language Arts
Grades:	3–5
Size:	Full class
Time:	30 minutes
Purpose:	To help children realize that others share the same fears and to help them cope with their fears.

Outcomes:

The students will be able to:
1. Identify the character's fear after listening to the story;
2. Discuss their own experiences with this fear;
3. Identify ways the character coped with his/her fear;
4. Generate ways of coping with this fear the next time it is encountered.

Materials:

A story selected from the *Bibliography of Children's Fears* (see Appendix C) or another story which addresses a childhood fear and in which the character(s) is able to cope with his/her fear.

Procedures:

1. Introduce the story and read it to the children. Ask them to listen for what the character(s) is afraid of and what the character(s) does when he/she is afraid.
2. Discuss the story with the children. Ask the children to talk about:
   a the character and what the character was afraid of;
   b. times they have experienced a similar fear;
   c. how they felt inside when they were afraid;
   d what the character did in the story to cope with his/her fear;
   e. what they do to help themselves when they are afraid;
   f. what they might do the next time they experience this fear.

Discussion of the story is the crucial part of this activity. It provides opportunities for students to share how they would feel, think and act in a similar situation and learn how the story character or other peers would cope with the same situation.

"Real Life" Fiction Writing

Fear:	Any Fear
Curricular Area:	Language Arts
Grades:	6–8
Size:	Full class
Time:	Several periods
Purpose:	To help students express and share anxieties and fears they may have experienced and explore alternative means of coping with them.
Outcomes:	*The students will be able to:*

1. Describe in written form a real fearful situation that they have encountered in their lives;
2. Share their experiences with their peers;
3. Fictionalize their real life experiences in short story form;
4. Devise alternative means of coping with fear inducing situations.

Materials: None

Procedures:

1. Assign students the task of writing down in detail the most frightening thing that has ever happened to them. Give examples of the kinds of things that may have happened to you or to others that you know about. Have the students discuss their own experiences as a pre-writing activity.
2. Share the real life stories with classmates the next day. Have students read their stories and ask questions of them to obtain further details. Allow enough time for all the students to share their stories.
3. Choose one real life story and, as a class, try to fictionalize the account as a model, following these steps:
   a. Make up names for the characters, describe what they look like, how they talk, where they are from, how old they are, etc. Decide on a point-of-view from which the story will be told.
   b. Describe the setting in detail, the time of year, the climate, etc.
   c. Explore plot alternatives, embellishing the story imaginatively with fictionalized details. Explore different resolutions of the problems encountered and choose the best solution.
4. Break the class into groups of 3 or 4 and have the group members brainstorm fictionalizations of each others' stories, following the model outlined above. Encourage group efforts to create exciting story lines.
5. Have each student write his own short story based on the fictionalized account of a real fearful event in his/her life.

6. Share the short stories with the entire class, either by duplicating and distributing them or having each student read his/hers to the class.

What Ifs...?

Fear:	Any Fear
Curricular Area:	Language Arts
Grades:	6–8
Size:	Full class
Time:	50 minutes
Purpose:	To help students understand the sources of anxiety and stress and generate ways to cope with setbacks and failures.
Outcomes:	*The students will be able to:* 1. Identify situations that may be sources of anxiety and stress; 2. Examine and describe a time when they tried something and failed; 3. Examine and describe a time when they were frightened, but took action and succeeded; 4. Discuss what they learned about trying, failing and coping with similar situations.
Materials:	1. Chalkboard or large sheet of newsprint 2. Marker 3. Worksheet: "Risky Business"

Procedures:	1. Write the following questions on the chalkboard or newsprint:
	   a What if I don't have anyone to eat lunch with?
	   b. What if I flunk the test?
	   c. What if I can't do the math homework?
	   d What if I don't get any A's?
	   e. What if I?
	2. Examine the "What if..." questions. Discuss how it is impossible to achieve our goals all the time without some setbacks and how sometimes we fall short of our expectations and have to muster the courage to start again.
	3. Brainstorm other "What if...?" problems/challenges. Record them on the board or newsprint.
	4. Have each student individually complete the worksheet, "Risky Business."
	5. Allow time to discuss generally situations that make one hesitate to act and some of the students' experiences in failing and succeeding in achieving their goals.

Risky Business

1. Describe a time when you decided that you'd rather do nothing than risk failure.

2. Describe a time when you took action, even though you were scared, and succeeded.

3. Describe a time when you tried something and failed. What did you learn from the experience?

4. What have you learned in general about trying, failing and gaining courage to try again?

The Worry Game

Fear:	New School
Curricular Area:	Social Studies
Grades:	6–8
Size:	Full Class
Time:	30 minutes
Purpose:	To help children realize that other students share anxieties about being in a new school setting and help them cope with those fears.
Outcomes:	*The students will be able to:*

1. Identify some worries associated with being in a new school setting;
2. Make decisions about coping strategies to deal with new school settings.

Materials: None

Procedures:

1. Divide the group into two teams, the **Worriers** and the **Doers**. The task of the Worrier team is to suggest things that might go wrong, be scary or cause worry on the first day of school. The task of the Doer team is to suggest solutions to the problems posed by the Worrier team members. If the problem is something for which there is no solution, then the Doers must suggest how a student could make the best of it.
2. Begin the game with the sentence: "Tomorrow is your first day in a new school."
3. Have the first Worrier team member make a suggestion of what might go wrong, be scary or cause worry. Collaboration is encouraged.
4. Have the first Doer team member provide a suggestion or decision to overcome the worry. Collaboration is encouraged.
5. If the Doer can make a reasonable suggestion (the teacher can be the judge), then the Doer team gets a point. If not, then the Worrier team gets a point. Continue on until all team members have had a chance to articulate a concern or a solution.
6. If time permits, have the teams switch roles. The team with the most points wins.

Using Children's Literature

Fear:	Any Fear
Curricular Area:	Language Arts
Grades:	6–8
Size:	Full class
Time:	30 minutes
Purpose:	To help children realize that others share the same fears and to help them cope with their fears.
Outcomes:	*The students will be able to:*

Outcomes: *The students will be able to:*
1. Identify the character's fear after reading stories or books;
2. Discuss their own experiences with this fear;
3. Identify ways the character coped with his/her fear;
4. Generate ways of coping with this fear the next time it is encountered.

Materials: A story or book selected from the *Bibliography of Children's Fears* (see Appendix C) or another story which addresses a childhood fear and in which the character(s) is able to cope with his/her fear.

Procedures:
1. Allow students to choose a story, book or chapter in a book which deals with a specific fearful situation. Ask them to notice what the character(s) is afraid of and what the character(s) does when he/she is afraid.
2. Discuss the story with the students. Ask the students to talk about:
   a. the character and what the character was afraid of;
   b. times they have experienced a similar fear;
   c. how they felt inside when they were afraid;
   d what the character did in the story to cope with his/her fear;
   e. what they do to help themselves when they are afraid;
   f. what they might do the next time they experience this fear.

Discussion of the stories or books is the crucial part of this activity. It provides opportunities for students to share how they would feel, think and act in a similar situation and learn how the story character or other peers would cope with the same situation.

Section 3

Fear Prevention Activities

Success A Day

Prevention:	Self-worth
Curricular Area:	Closure activity for any area of curriculum
Grades:	K–8
Size:	Full class or individual
Time:	15 minutes
Purpose:	To help students feel more self-confident by recognizing their daily achievements.
Outcomes:	*The students will be able to:*

1. Identify one success they experienced that day;
2. Share a success with the class.

Materials:	None

Procedures:

1. Take 10–15 minutes at the end of a class period or the end of the school day for each student to share one success or achievement he/she experienced that day.
2. If a student finds this difficult at first, or says he/she has had no success, ask other students to think of a success or accomplishment they witnessed the student achieve. The teacher should also be aware of students' successes during the day.
3. A variation of this activity is to have each student share with the class one thing he/she feels he/she learned that day.

Source: Canfield, J., & Wells, H. C. (1976). *100 ways to enhance self-concept in the classroom.* Englewood Cliffs, N.J: Prentice-Hall, Inc.

Classroom Meetings

Prevention:	Control, Security, Self-worth
Curricular Area:	Any area
Grades:	K–8
Size:	Full class
Time:	20–40 minutes
Purpose:	To enhance communication between students and teacher, promote problem-solving skills and encourage students to take responsibility for planning classroom goals and activities.
Outcomes:	*The students will be able to:*

The students will be able to:
1. Identify the purpose of holding class meetings;
2. List rules and procedures for conducting class meetings;
3. Participate in a class meeting.

Materials: None

Procedures:

1. Class meetings are opportunities for students to work cooperatively to plan and make decisions about classroom rules and activities and solve problems that arise within the class.
2. Discuss the concept of class meetings with the students. Decide what the purpose of the class meetings will be and what topics will be discussed. Examples:

    Field trip ideas
    Classroom chores
    Rules and consequences for classroom behavior
    Playground problems
    Ideas for projects

3. Suggested guidelines for class meetings:
    a. Each member should have an equal vote;
    b. A chairperson and recorder should preside at each meeting;
    c. A definite day or time each week should be set;
    d. A person must raise one's hand to be recognized;
    e. Only those things that are the business of the class should be topics for discussion;
    f. An agenda box can be set up for students to provide written agenda items;
    g. Decisions are binding, and any alternatives or changes must wait until the next meeting.

4. Suggested procedure for class meetings:
    a. Chairperson calls the meeting to order;
    b. Read meeting rules and decisions from the previous meeting;
    c. Discuss any unfinished business;
    d. Discuss only agenda items;
    e. Take a vote and let the majority rule.

Brainstorming

Prevention:	Security, Control
Curricular Area:	Social Studies, Language Arts
Grades:	K–2
Size:	Full class
Time:	20 minutes
Purpose:	To help students develop critical thinking skills and recognize that there are many solutions to a situation or many ways of doing the same thing.

Outcomes: *The students will be able to:*
1. Generate many solutions or ideas for the same situation;
2. Recognize that different people approach a situation in a variety of ways.

Materials:
1. Clock or watch with second hand
2. Chart or board

Procedures:
1. Explain to the students that there are many ways of doing the same thing. In this activity, you would like them to suggest as many solutions to a situation as possible within the time limit set. Tell them that thinking of as many things as possible in a certain period of time is called "Brainstorming."
2. Allow about 3-4 minutes for each topic. Select two or three topics from the suggestions below. (The remaining topics may be used for a second lesson on brainstorming or later as readiness exercises for other problem-solving activities).
3. The rules for brainstorming are quite simple:

   - Students are to suggest (in an orderly fashion) as many solutions to the problem as they can come up with during the time set aside for suggestions.
   - During the suggestions phase, students may not comment on the quality or feasibility of the solutions. The goal is to get as many ideas out as possible.
   - Record the solutions suggested on a board or chart. Model an accepting attitude and resist any efforts on the part of students to "put down" someone else's ideas. Comment on the number of ideas and creativity shown by the students.

   Suggested topics for Brainstorming:
   a. How can you make friends with a new person at school?
   b. How can you decide who will be first in a game?
   c. How can you help your teacher?
   d. How can you show your mother or father you love him/her?
   e. What can you do to entertain yourself if you are home alone?
   f. What can you do during a frightening thunderstorm?

g. What can you do if you get lost?
h. What can you do if you are near a dog or other animal you are afraid of?

Source: Chiak, M. K., & Heron, B. J. (1980). *Games children should play*. Glenview, IL: Scott Foresman & Co.

Feelings Ensemble

Prevention:	Security, Control
Curricular Areas:	Language Arts, Music
Grades:	K–2
Size:	Full class, groups
Time:	30–40 minutes
Purpose:	To help students identify their feelings and how they communicate them to other people.

Outcomes: *The students will be able to:*
1. Name some feeling words;
2. Listen to a poem and identify feeling words;
3. Create a musical composition with rhythm instruments that expresses a feeling;
4. Describe times when they feel the feelings expressed in the music.

Materials:
1. Rhythm instruments (self-made or purchased)
2. Chart or chalkboard
3. Poem **"It's All Right to Cry"** (attached)

Procedures:
1. Introduce the word **"feelings"** and ask the students to name some feelings and record their responses on a chart or blackboard.
2. Tell the students you are going to read a poem, and you would like them to listen for the feelings in the poem.
3. Read the poem **"It's All Right to Cry"** once or twice. Record any additional feelings mentioned on the chart or board.
4. Divide the students into groups of 4 or 5 and give each member of the group a different instrument. Explain that you will secretly give each group a feeling word and they can make up a short song to express that feeling. The other groups will guess which feeling is being expressed by each group's performance. The song need only be 30 seconds to a minute long. The following feeling words lend themselves to this activity:

afraid	*happy*	*angry*
sad	*excited*	*nervous*
lonely		

5. As each feeling composition is guessed, ask the students to tell about times when they feel that way.

Source: Bowman, R. P. (1987). Approaches for counseling children through music. *Elementary School Guidance & Counseling, 21*(4), 284, 289.

It's All Right to Cry

It's all right to cry
Crying gets the sad out of you.
It's all right to cry
It might make you feel better.

Raindrops from your eyes
Washing all the mad out of you.
Raindrops from you eyes
It might make you feel better.

It's all right to feel things
Though the feelings may be strange.
Feelings are such real things
And they change and change and change.
Sad and grumpy,
Down in the dumpy,
Snuggly huggly
Mean and ugly
Sloppy slappy
Hoppy happy
Change and change and change...

It's all right to know
Feelings come and go,
And it's all right to cry
It might make you feel better.

by Carol Hall

How I've Grown

Prevention:	Self-worth
Curricular Areas:	Science, Math, Social Studies, Language Arts
Grades:	K–2
Size:	Full class, individual
Time:	60 minutes
Purpose:	To help students increase their awareness that they are unique because of their different interests and physical abilities.

Outcomes:

The students will be able to:
1. Identify ways they have changed and grown;
2. Name likenesses and differences between themselves and others;
3. Identify how their interests have changed;
4. Match each picture with the correct name.

Materials:

1. Bulletin board
2. Photograph of each student at a younger age
3. Yarn
4. Push pins
5. Scrapbook (optional)
6. Name cards

Procedures:

1. Ask the children to bring an earlier childhood picture (photo) of themselves and a current picture (This could be taken at school by the children or an adult).
2. Prepare a bulletin board entitled "How I've Grown." Under the current picture, place a name card with a length of colorful yarn. Place early childhood pictures randomly on the bulletin board. Be sure children's names are on the back of their pictures.
3. Give the children an opportunity to view the pictures and match them (younger with present day) using the yarn.
4. Discuss what they observed and how they changed:
   a. What differences among each other do you see?
   b. What likenesses among each other do you see?
   c. How have you changed from your earlier picture to now?
   d. What did you like to do at that younger age?
   e. What do you like to do now?

Optional: If this activity is done early in the year, the pictures can be placed in a scrapbook (one child's picture per page.) Late in the year, take pictures again and make comparisons. A short story could be be written about how they have changed.

Workers in the Dark

Prevention:	Control
Curricular Areas:	Social Studies, Language Art, Reading, Art
Grades:	K–2
Size:	Full class, group, or individual
Time:	60–90 minutes
Purpose:	To help children gain a sense of security and control by realizing that many adults perform their jobs at night or in the dark.
Outcome:	*The students will be able to:*

1. Identify jobs that people perform in the dark or at night;
2. Demonstrate through role playing how people who work in the dark perform their job;
3. Draw a picture of symbols of jobs people perform in the dark;
4. Match the symbol with the name of the job to which it corresponds.

Materials:

1. Heavy weight drawing paper, 5.5 x 8 inch.
2. Crayons or markers

Procedures:

1. Introduce the activity by asking the children to name their parents' jobs. Ask if they can think of jobs that people perform at night or in the dark. Some possibilities include:

photography processor	*mine*
firefighter	*deep sea diver*
night security	*police*
astronaut	*astronomer*
paramedics	*doctors / nurses*

2. Locate (or have the children locate) books in the library about jobs that are performed in the dark or at night. Read to the children (or have them read in small groups) to find out more about those jobs. Discuss the environment they work in and why it is necessary for them to work in the dark.
3. Give each child an opportunity to role play one of the jobs and let the other students guess which job it is.
4. Provide paper and crayons or markers. Ask the students to draw a picture or symbol of the jobs discussed. Try to make sure each job is represented by a symbol or picture.
5. Print (or have the students print) the name of each job on another 5.5 x 8 heavy piece of paper. Use the pictures and job names to play a matching game like concentration. Place all cards face down. Taking turns, turn two over at a time. If they match, that student keeps the cards. If they don't match, they are turned back over in their place. This last activity can be used for individual or small group reinforcement.

Family Pictures

Prevention:	Security, Self-worth
Curricular Areas:	Language Arts, Social Studies, Science, Art
Grades:	K–2
Size:	Full class
Time:	90–120 minutes
Purpose:	To help the students recognize that people are organized into families and that each family is unique.
Outcomes:	*The students will be able to:*

1. Name a variety of living things;
2. Classify the living things into groups or categories;
3. Draw a picture of their own family and label each member;
4. Discuss an activity that their family does together.

Materials:

1. Magazines that include as many different pictures as possible of people, animals, and plants
2. Drawing paper
3. Crayons, markers or paint
4. Chalkboard or chart
5. Scissors
6. Glue

Procedures:

1. Discuss the meaning of the term "alive" with the children. Ask the students to name living things and list them on the board.
2. Provide magazines and ask the children to cut out pictures of many different living things.
3. Gather the children into a large group or small groups with their pictures. They can form a circle and spread their pictures out in the middle of the circle.
4. Ask the children to look over their pictures and decide if any of the pictures could go together in families. They may first say all the plants should go together in one family and the animals in another. Accept this, but encourage finer classification, such as classifying into dog family, tree family, fish family, human family, etc.
5. Group the pictures according to the family classifications determined. Let each child participate.
6. In small groups, glue each classification or family of pictures on a large enough sheet of paper. Label each family and write one sentence about each one. Display in the room or on a bulletin board.
7. As a follow-up to the above activity, ask the students to draw a picture of their own family, including each member. Ask them or help them to label each member.

8. Gather the children into a group to talk about their family. Suggestions include:
   a. *Who is in your family?*
   b. *Name something your family does together.*
   c. *What are families for?*
   d. *Are all the families in the class alike?*
   e. *What does your family do for you?*
   f. *What do you do for your family?*

Family Visitors

Prevention:	Security, Self-worth
Curricular Areas:	Social Studies, Language Arts
Grades:	K–2
Size:	Full class
Time:	20–30 minutes per visit
Purpose:	To help the students recognize the importance of their own family and the uniqueness of each family.
Outcomes:	*The students will be able to:*

1. Answer questions and communicate with other students about their (own) family;
2. Identify ways in which families are similar and different;
3. List reasons why families are important.

Materials:
1. Long sheet of paper (vertical or horizontal)
2. Marker

Procedures:
1. Schedule times throughout the year for each child to invite one or more members of his/her family to visit the classroom and to talk about their family. A suggestion is to send a letter home at the beginning of the year explaining this project.
2. Before a visit, have the students draw up questions that they may wish to ask the visitors to talk about, such as:
   a. the families favorite foods
   b. what the family does for fun
   c. how they share responsibilities
   d. different places they have lived
3. When a family visits, encourage the student and his/her family member(s) to bring pictures or other items that may represent the family.
4. After each visit, list one or two reasons why families are important on a long paper labeled "WHY FAMILIES ARE IMPORTANT." Some examples follow:

   Families take care of each other
   Families live together
   Families have fun together
   Families celebrate birthdays

5. The teacher should be sure to schedule a visit by his/her own family.

Peruvian Worry Dolls

Prevention:	Security, Control
Curricular Areas:	Art, Social Studies, Language Arts,
Grades:	K–4
Size:	Full class
Time:	Several periods
Purpose:	To reduce the effects of fears and stress through communication and release.
Outcome:	*The students will be able to:*

Outcome: *The students will be able to:*
1. Construct simple dolls of paper or other materials;
2. Verbalize and communicate their fears;
3. Achieve cathartic release of their fears and stress.

Materials: Varies according to the complexity of the doll making.

Procedures:
1. Among a number of the native peoples of Peru, children make "Worry Dolls"—one for each day of the week. The dolls are usually small, but they can be of any size. In Peru, they are often carved from corn husks or made from burlap, but any material (paper, paper mache, straws, etc.) can be used.
2. A child makes one doll for each day of the week. Each evening the child gets down the doll for that day and tells the doll his or her troubles and worries. Such an activity helps children begin to verbalize those things that cause them stress and fear. The cathartic release of verbalizing one's worries is often therapeutic in and of itself. It allows for reflection and helps the child listen to himself/herself. It is similar to the effects of journal or diary writing.
3. One variation would be to suggest that the children record their talks to the worry dolls and periodically play the tapes back to themselves for their own benefit and reflection.

Reducing Test Stress

Prevention:	Self-worth, Security, Control
Curricular Area:	Any area
Grades:	2–6
Size:	Full class
Time:	60 minutes
Purpose:	To help reduce students' anxiety about taking standardized tests and build their confidence in developing test-taking strategies to assist them.

Outcomes: *The students will be able to:*
1. Identify ways to prepare themselves for taking a test;
2. Role play and practice some test-taking strategies to use during a test;
3. Take tests with less anxiety.

Materials:
1. Teacher made sample tests
2. Paper
3. #2 pencils

Procedures:
1. Preparing ahead of time to do well on a test includes eating a good breakfast or healthy food, getting a good night's rest, practicing relaxation exercises and bringing materials needed for the test to school.
2. Students can make their own simple graph chart to keep records or check off each way to prepare for a test.
3. Students will feel more secure about taking a test if they practice test-taking strategies that put them in control of the testing situation.
4. Teach the following strategies. Use role playing of each strategy as well as actual practice on teacher made practice tests to reinforce learning of strategies.
   a. Listen to or read test directions carefully. (The teacher can read directions for the students to follow and provide written directions to read and follow.)
   b. Make your best guess. Eliminate answers you know are wrong by crossing them out and look for any clues in the remaining answers to help you decide.
   c. If the test must be completed in a certain amount of time, work at a medium pace and do not spend too much time on one question. Be sure to allow time to answer questions you know.
   d. If time allows, be sure to double check your answers to make sure nothing is left out.
   e. Breathe slowly and remain calm throughout the test.
5. The more practice the students experience, the easier it will be for them to use the strategies in a test-taking situation.

Architects

Prevention:	Control, Security, Self-worth
Curricular Areas:	Language Arts, Science, Art, Social Studies
Grades:	2-8
Size:	Full class
Time:	30 minutes
Purpose:	To help the students experience working together and communicating with others non-verbally.
Outcomes:	*The students will be able to:*

1. Construct a structure using straws or tinker toys within a time limit;
2. Work and cooperate with others in small groups;
3. Communicate non-verbally with other group members;
4. Evaluate their ability to perform outcomes 1, 2 and 3 above.

Materials: Tinker toys or straws and tape

Procedures:

1. Divide the students into groups of no more than 5 or 6 students. Give each group the same amount of tinker toys or straws and tape. Explain to them that they have 15 minutes to build a structure together. They may not speak to each other, but they may communicate non-verbally.
2. You can give each group a total number of points for following directions, completing a structure and communicating non-verbally and subtract points for verbal communication. Explain this carefully before you begin.
3. When the time limit is up, allow time to evaluate the activity. Discuss the following:
   a. how they communicated non-verbally;
   b. if people worked separately or together;
   c. how they feel about their structure;
   d. behaviors that get in the way of group cooperation;
   e. how they worked within the group;
   f. what contributes to successful team work.

Me Tree

Prevention:	Self-esteem
Curricular Areas:	Social Studies, Language Arts
Grades:	3–5
Size:	Full class
Time:	60 minutes
Purpose:	To enhance students' self-esteem by helping students recognize their talents and how they use them.
Outcomes:	*The students will be able to:* 1. Identify and record their talents and abilities; 2. Record specific ways each talent is used; 3. Share and discuss a talent and the way it is used with the rest of the class; 4. Observe that people are different and that each has worthwhile abilities.
Materials:	1. "Me Tree" handout 2. Pencil 3. Crayons
Procedures:	1. Introduce the activity by discussing talents and accomplishments in general. Use examples of talented people. 2. Brainstorm and write a list on the board of talents and how they are used. Some examples include:

Coordination	*Play baseball* *Swim on a team*
Musical talent	*Play an instrument*
Artistic talent	*Draw pictures for others*

3. Distribute the "Me Tree" handout.
4. Instruct the students to write their talents on the roots and their accomplishments on the branches.
5. Let the students share their "Me Trees" with the group.

Source: Lesesne, T. S. (1980). *I'm special.* Charlotte, NC: The Drug Education Center.

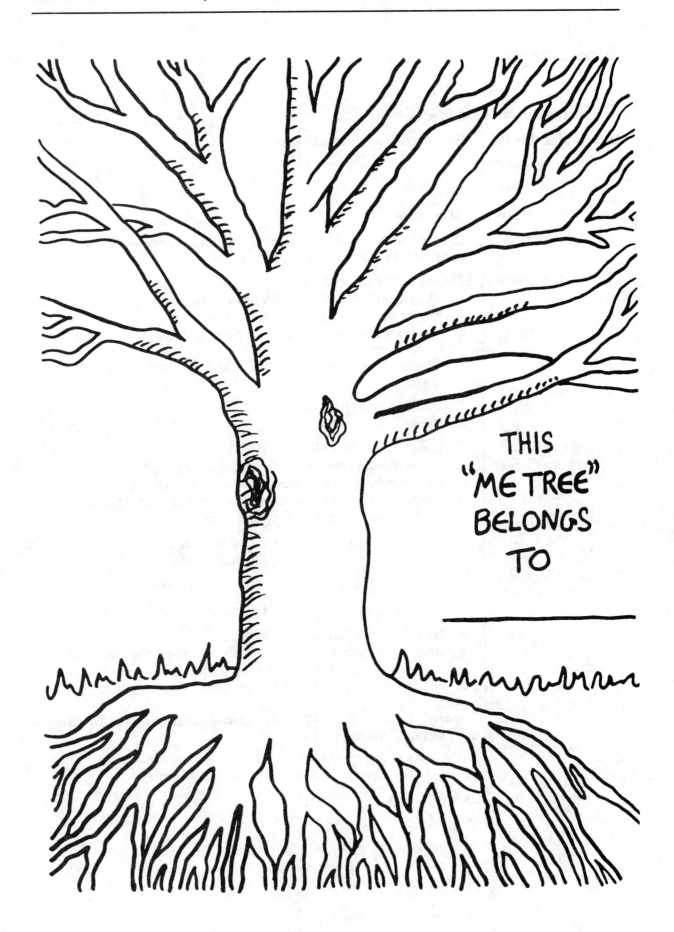

THIS "ME TREE" BELONGS TO

Diamante

Prevention:	Self-worth
Curricular Areas:	Language Arts, Reading
Grades:	3–5
Size:	Full class
Time:	50 minutes
Purpose:	To help increase their awareness that they are unique because of their different interests, abilities and feelings.
Outcome:	*The students will be able to:* 1. Write a diamante describing themselves; 2. Share their diamantes with other students; 3. Illustrate their diamantes; 4. Identify likenesses and differences between themselves and others.
Materials:	1. Paper and pencil 2. Drawing paper 12" by 18" 3. Markers or crayons
Procedures:	1. A diamante is a poetic form that has seven lines and takes the shape of a diamond. Example:

Lucy
happy, successful
playing video games, swimming, iceskating
a fourth grade student at Robinson International School
writing reports, playing field hockey, cooking
good, satisfied
Jackson

Line 1: First name
Line 2: Two adjectives that describe how you feel about school
Line 3: Three verbs telling what you like to do
Line 4: A phrase to connect the other lines (write this one last)
Line 5: Three verbs telling what you are good at
Line 6: Two adjectives that describe how you feel about yourself
Line 7: Last name

2. Give the students an example and teach them the form of a diamante. Providing the student with a form would be helpful. Write a sample diamante with the class.

3. Allow time for the students to write a diamante about themselves.
4. When the students have finished writing their diamante, ask them to glue their diamante to one half of a 12 inch by 18 inch drawing paper. Then illustrate a word or phrase from the diamante on the other half of the paper.
5. Allow time for the students to read their diamantes to the class.

Source: Practical ideas for counselors, 9(4), March/April 1988.

Feeling Masks

Prevention:	Security, Control
Curricular Areas:	Art, Social Studies, Language Arts
Grades:	3–5
Size:	Full class
Time:	60–180 minutes
Purpose:	To help students realize that we have many different feelings and recognize how we communicate our feelings to others.
Outcome:	*The students will be able to:* 1. Listen to a poem and identify feeling words; 2. Name a variety of feelings people have; 3. Create a feeling mask; 4. Identify what causes feelings and role play how we act when we feel different ways.
Materials:	1. The Poem, "I Have Feelings." 2. Materials for masks: See the following page.
Procedures:	1. This activity can be carried out as simply or as involved as the teacher may choose. The main idea is to make feeling masks using paper plates, paper bags or paper mache. 2. Read the poem, "I Have Feelings" to the students. Ask the students to listen for feelings that are mentioned in the poem:

I Have Feelings

I have feelings and you do too,
I'd like to share a few with you.
Sometimes I'm happy and sometimes I'm sad,
Sometimes I'm scared, and sometimes I'm mad.
The most important feeling, you see,
Is that I'm proud of being me.

No one sees the things I see;
Behind my eyes is only me.
And no one knows where my feelings begin,
For there's only me inside my skin.
No one knows what I can do;
I'll be me, and you be you.

It's a wonderful thing how everyone owns,
Just enough skin to cover his bones.
My dad's would be too big to fit;
I'd be all wrinkled inside of it.
Baby sister's would be much too small;
It wouldn't cover me up at all.
I feel just right in the skin I wear—
There's no one like me anywhere.

3. As the students name the feelings they heard or any other feelings people have, write them on a board or chart. Some feeling words that will work well with the mask-making activity are:

    happy   *sad*   *angry*
    excited   *afraid*   *brave*
    proud

4. Explain to the students they will be making masks that show these feelings. The type of masks being made will determine the demonstration. The masks can be made individually or by small groups working together.

5. When the masks have been completed, use them with the students in a large group or in small groups to identify the time when we have these feelings, and act out with the mask what we do when we feel angry, sad, happy, etc.

6. The mask can be used throughout the year, and can also decorate an area of the classroom.

Masks and Materials

A. Paper Plate Masks

Paper plates
Scissors
Markers or crayons
Flat wooden sticks or string

Cut eyes in the plates and use markers or crayons to draw the facial expressions. A stick can be glued to the plate at the bottom to hold the plate to one's face or string can be attached at each side to tie it on.

B. Paper Bag Masks

Paper bags (brown or white)
Scissors
Markers, crayons or paints

Cut eyes in the bags and use markers, crayons or paints to create the face.

C. Paper Mache Masks

Paper (newspaper or newsprint)
Flour and water paste or glue
Balloons or some other curved form
Tempera paint

C. Paper Mache Masks (continued)

Brushes
Shellac or clear varnish

Tear paper into strips and dip in a flour paste mixture or glue-water mixture (thin, creamy consistency) for a minute or two until soaked. Layer the wet strips over half an inflated balloon or other curved form and build up to a one quarter inch thickness. Let dry completely. Trim edges, cut opening for eyes and use tempera paints to create the facial expression. The masks can be coated with a shellac or clear varnish to preserve them.

Where Do You Stand?

Prevention:	Control, Security
Curricular Areas:	Social Studies, Language Arts
Grades:	3-5
Size:	Full class
Time:	20 minutes
Purpose:	To help students realize that they do make decisions and recognize some influences over their decision making.
Outcome:	*The students will be able to:*

1. Decide whether to agree, disagree or not take a stand on certain issues;
2. Recognize that people hold different opinions about the same issue;
3. Identify influences that affect their decisions.

Materials:
1. Three 5 x 8 cards with the words "AGREE," "DISAGREE" and "NOT SURE" written on them
2. Masking tape

Procedures:
1. Introduce the activity by discussing what opinions are and how our opinions influence our decisions. Ask them to think about some of the decisions they made that morning while getting ready for school. Discuss how some decisions are easy to make and some are difficult.
2. Show the students the AGREE, DISAGREE and NOT SURE cards and post them on different walls in the room. Explain to the students that you will read a statement, and they should stand near the card that describes what they decide about the statement. Have them gather in the center of the room.
3. Some suggested statements are:
   a. People can be judged by the clothes they wear.
   b. It is easier to receive a compliment than give one.
   c. Girls should be allowed to play any sports.
   d. There is too much violence on TV.
   e. It is hard to believe something when your friends think you are wrong.
   f. School should be more work than fun.
   g. It's not fair to have a birthday party and invite everyone in your class except for two or three people.
4. When the students take their stands, solicit reasons for their decisions from each of the three groups.
5. Discuss the activity with the students using the following questions as a guide:
   a. Did you agree with your friends all the time?
   b. Did you hear other people's opinions?

   c. Why were some issues easy to take a stand on and others difficult?
   d. How do we go about making decisions?
   e. What factors influence our decisions?

Source: Lesesne, T. S. (1980). *I'm special.* Charlotte, NC: The Drug Education Center.

Families at Work

Prevention:	Control, Security
Curricular Areas:	Social Studies, Language Arts
Grades:	3–5
Size:	Full class
Time:	30–40 minutes per visit
Purpose:	To help the students realize that families work together to support each other and help them learn to become independent adults.
Outcomes:	*The students will be able to:* 1. Identify how the jobs and careers of family members contribute to the family; 2. Name some rewards that a family experiences because of the work family members perform; 3. Identify ways that their work contributes to the good of the family; 4. Recognize similarities and differences in the work their families perform.
Materials:	None

Procedures:	1. Schedule times throughout the year for each child to invite one or more members of his/her family to visit the classroom to talk about their career or work. A suggestion is to send a letter home at the beginning of the year explaining this project.
	2. Before the first visit, have the students find some information in the library or elsewhere on various jobs/careers. Ask them to think about questions they may want to ask the visitor about his/her job, such as:
	  a. What is your training?
	  b. What are your hours?
	  c. What are your responsibilities?
	  d. What do you like and not like about your work?
	  e. What kind of special equipment do you use?
	3. Encourage the visitors to bring any special equipment, tools, or other items representative of their work. Discuss with the class and visitor(s) how the work they do outside the home contributes to the family. What fun things can the family enjoy because of the jobs that family members have?
	4. As a follow-up to any visit, have the children write their own resume listing jobs and work that they perform. Discuss how their work contributes to the family.

Journal Writing

Prevention:	Self-worth
Curricular Area:	Language Arts
Grades:	3–8
Size:	Full class
Time:	30 minutes (throughout year)
Purpose:	To help students build their self confidence by exploring through writing their thoughts, feelings, successes and failures.
Outcomes:	*The students will be able to:*

1. Express in writing personal thoughts and feelings;
2. Identify their strengths and weaknesses;
3. Record personal growth throughout the year.

Materials: Standard-sized composition notebook or binder and lined looseleaf paper

Procedures:

1. Introduce the journal as similar to a diary. It is a private book of thoughts and feelings. It is not meant to be shared with anyone—not with teachers, parents or other students. Tell the students that sometimes they may want to invite someone to read a page of their journal. Explain that they will be able to write in their journals regularly and as the months go by, it will be interesting to look back in the journal to see how their feelings and thoughts have changed.
2. Encourage students to design appropriate covers, reflecting the interests and talents of each owner.
3. Sample introduction of first entry:

   "Feelings are sometimes difficult to talk about. They get jumbled up inside of us. Writing about our feelings sometimes helps us understand ourselves better. Lets think for a few minutes about how we feel right now."

   Provide an example such as:

   "Right now, I'm feeling two feelings at once. I'm feeling proud because you did such fine work this morning, and I'm feeling excited about beginning journal writing."

4. Ask the students to open their journal to the first page, write the date and begin the journal.
5. Explain that journal writing is private writing; it is always done in silence.
6. It is important that the teacher keep a journal and use this time to record his/her entry. The teacher may want to provide journal writing time daily, twice weekly, or once a week.

7. Teachers may want to use some of the suggestions for journal entries on the next page.

Source: Chiak, M. K., & Heron, B. J. (1980). *Games children should play.* Glenview, IL: Scott Foresman & Co.

Additional Suggestions for Journal Entries

Self-awareness:

I'm feeling _____ because I _____ and I'd like to _____.

I feel angry when _____.

I would be happier if _____.

I used to be_____. Now I _____.

I wonder about _____.

I worry about _____.

I'm glad I _____.

I'm sorry I _____.

Self image:

Some things that I like about myself are _____.

I'm proud of myself because _____.

If I could be anything I wanted to be, I would be _____.

I wish I could _____.

I can _____.

Goal Setting:

I want to learn _____.

Today I made progress in _____.

By next month I hope to learn to _____.

In ten years I hope to _____.

One thing I'd really like to change about myself is _____.

I'll start changing by _____.

Journal Reflection:

When I read my journal, I learned that _____.

When I read my journal, I remembered _____.

Something I noticed about myself when I read my journal is _____.

Senoian Dream Work

Prevention:	Control, Security
Curricular Areas:	Creative Writing, Art, Drama
Grades:	4–8
Size:	Groups
Time:	45 minutes
Purpose:	To help students deal with their fears through creative expression.
Outcomes:	*The students will be able to:*

1. Recall and relate their dreams to their peers;
2. Create art, stories or plays based on materials from their dreams;
3. Gain support from their peers in dealing with fears expressed in dreams;
4. Cope better with the fears expressed in their dreams.

Materials:	Drawing paper, colored pencils, pens, paints, writing paper
Procedures:	

1. Dreams can be used educationally as material for creative writing, drama and art projects while at the same time providing catharsis for the fears which emerge during our sleeping hours. The following instructions can be read to the class as a beginning to a set of creative activities dealing with dreams:

   "Dreams are important because they give us access to material that is not available while we are awake. At night, when our defenses are down, our emotions express themselves freely and in strange ways. Negative emotions, such as fear, anger and hostility, often leave the greatest impression on us as nightmares. However, the dream world is also a place where positive emotions express themselves, and if we can find ways of understanding this information, it can enrich our waking hours.

   The Senoi [rhymes with annoy] are a people who live in the Central Malay Peninsula. They believe that dreams are very important, and they are taught from a very young age how to work with their dreams. When they wake up after a dream, they often try to continue the dream in their imagination, talk to some of the characters in their dreams and finish what was left unfinished. If they dream of falling, for example, they imagine that they are falling to some place and that they land safely, and they look around to see what they can learn from this place. If they dream that a frightening stranger chases them, in their imagination they turn around and confront the stranger and ask the person what he or she wants, or what he or she is trying to tell them.

Now I'd like for all of you to get into groups of about three or four, and if you're comfortable talking about some of your dreams, see what you can remember, and perhaps some of you have some of the same experiences in your dreams. Ask yourselves how the dreams made you feel? Perhaps you will want to go in your imagination back to a dream and talk with someone in the dream, or continue the dream and see where it leads."

2. As extensions of this exercise, have students do some of the following:
   a. Write a short story using their dream as the starting point;
   b. Draw a picture or a story board of a dream and its resolution;
   c. Make a group painting of a dream;
   d. Make up a skit or short play about one of the group member's dreams.

Source: Clower, G. *A pilot counseling project for preadolescent girls.* Unpublished paper.

Win, Lose, Draw

Prevention:	Security
Curricular Area:	Any Content Area
Grades:	4–8
Size:	Full class, groups
Time:	30–40 minutes
Purpose:	To help the students experience working together as a group.
Outcomes:	*The students will be able to:*

The students will be able to:
1. Communicate with each other verbally and non-verbally to identify a word or phrase;
2. Evaluate what behaviors are needed to work cooperatively in a group.

Materials:
1. Vocabulary words or phrases from any content area written on small pieces of paper
2. Chalk board and chalk or chart and marker
3. Clock with second hand or other type of timer

Procedures:
1. This game is similar to charades or Pictionary. Divide the class into two teams. Explain to the students that one team member at a time is given a paper with a word or phrase written on it. The team member draws symbols or pictures to give the other members of the team clues about the word. Letters of the alphabet or numbers may not be a part of the drawings, but parts of the word may be written on the board or chart as they are guessed. The person drawing may not speak, but other team members may call out their guesses as they think of them.
2. The time limit is usually 3 minutes, but this may be adjusted to the group. If the team guesses the word or phrase within the time limit, they will receive a point. If not, the other team may make one guess and if correct, they receive a point. Play is alternated between the two teams.
3. After each team has had an equal number of turns, discuss what helped each team to successfully guess the words or phrases. What hindered them?

This is a good game for introducing or reinforcing vocabulary words.

Cooperative Outdoor Games

Prevention:	Security, Control, Self-worth
Curricular Areas:	Physical Education, Social Studies, Language Arts
Grades:	4–8
Size:	Full class or small group
Time:	5–10 minutes per activity
Purpose:	To help students improve their communication and problem-solving skills through participation in cooperative games.
Outcomes:	*The students will be able to:*

1. Cooperate with other students in small groups to complete a task;
2. Communicate verbally and non-verbally with other students in a small group;
3. Assess a problem, generate possible solutions in a small group and participate in making a group decision;
4. Offer support and encouragement to each other in a small group to complete a task.

Materials:
1. Balls (kick ball size)
2. Small platform or sturdy table

Procedures:

The following activities generally require a large open space. Exercise caution to limit the risk of injury during these activities. Describe the nature of the activity to be attempted and provide a demonstration when appropriate. One suggestion for grouping students into smaller groups or pairs is by birthday months.

1. ***Lap Ball:*** All players sit in a very close circle, shoulder to shoulder, legs stretched straight out in front. The object of the game is to pass the ball from lap to lap around the circle X number of times without using hands. A large group could be divided into two groups to see which group can pass it most quickly.

2. ***Pass and Catch:*** Have the players line up in two parallel lines, each facing another person, about 10 feet (3 meters) apart. The first person in one line throws the ball to the person directly opposite him or her, then runs to the end of his/her respective line, and the next person quickly moves up. Repeat the entire line as many times as desired.

3. ***All Aboard:*** This requires a small platform or sturdy table not quite big enough to accommodate the group. Ask all members to get on the platform and stay on it for 5 seconds.

4. **Stand Up:** With a partner, players sit back to back, arms interlocked at the elbows with knees bent. The object is to stand up. A variation of this activity is to try it with 3, 4 or 5 players.

5. ***Python Pentathlon:*** All group members are seated on the floor in a line, and each student puts his or her legs around the waist of the person in front. The group is then instructed to move to a pre-determined point.

6. ***Knots:*** All players stand in a circle, shoulder to shoulder, and then grasp hands, one with each hand. Players are not to grasp the hands of the persons next to them. Then, untie the knot without anyone letting go of the hands that he/she holds. Pivoting of hands without breaking the grasp is permissible.

7. ***Four Pointers:*** The object is to get the group to move from Point A to Point B with only six supporting points (feet, arms or knees) touching the ground. Distance to be traveled, number of supporting points and number in each group can be varied depending on the skill and skill level of the group.

Source: Duncan, K., Beck, D. L., & Granum, R. A. (1988). Project explore: An activity-based counseling group. *The School Counselor, 35*(3), 215–219.

African Shield

Prevention:	Self-worth
Curricular Areas:	Social Studies, Art
Grades:	6–8
Size:	Full class
Time:	60–90 minutes
Purpose:	To help students build their self-confidence by identifying significant events, achievements and successes unique to them.
Outcome:	*The students will be able to:*

Outcome: *The students will be able to:*
1. Express in literal drawing or symbols significant events, achievements and successes unique to them;
2. Share with other members of the group a personal success or achievement.

Materials:
1. African Shield Handout
2. Crayons, markers or paint

Procedures:
1. Introduce the activity and ask the students to create their individual shields by expressing the following events or accomplishments in drawings or symbols:
   a. The most significant event in your life so far.
   b. Your greatest achievement in the past year.
   c. Your happiest moment in the past month.
   d. Something you are good at.
   e. Something you are striving to become.
   f. Something you did well this week.
   g. If you died today, three words you would most like to be said of you.
2. When the students have finished creating their shields, allow time for each student to share one or two areas of their shields with the class or allow them to share their entire shield with a small group of students.

Source: Canfield, J., & Wells, H.C. (1976). *100 ways to enhance self-concept in the classroom.* Englewood Cliffs, NJ: Prentice-Hall, Inc.

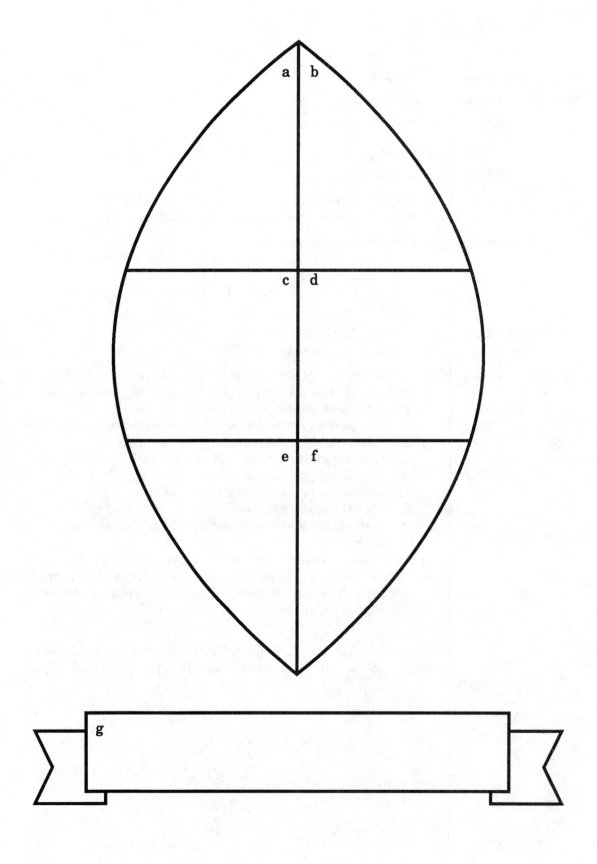

Validations

Prevention:	Self-worth
Curricular Area:	Language Arts
Grades:	6–8
Size:	Full class
Time:	30–40 minutes
Purpose:	To help students appreciate the positive qualities of others as well as recognize positive qualities that others see in them.
Outcomes:	*The students will be able to:*

1. Identify and write one positive quality for each member of the class;
2. Recognize the positive qualities that others see in them;
3. Construct clear validation statements for each student.

Materials:
1. Plain white 8.5 x 11 inch paper
2. Thin point markers or pens
3. Masking tape

Procedures:
1. Introduce the activity to the students. Spend time discussing the following points:
   a. Sometimes it's difficult to give another person praise or a genuine compliment.
   b. To let people know what we appreciate and respect about them is to validate them—we express appreciation and approval in a positive way.
   c. Validation may be a new skill or a new idea. Sometimes it's easier to put someone down than to compliment them.
   d. As we become better at validating others, we can learn to be clearer about what we like or appreciate about each other. For example, if we say to a friend, "You're a nice person," that person may be complimented, but not clear about exactly what we mean. The validation is too fuzzy. But if we say, "I really enjoy or like your sense of humor," the person knows exactly what quality we appreciate. The validator is clear and specific.
   e. Emphasize the following differences between clear and fuzzy validations:

Fuzzy	**Clear**
You look good.	*I like the way your hair looks today.*
You're sweet.	*I like the way you always say something nice about other people.*

    f.   Suggest the following validation guidelines to the class. Try to start your validations with "I":

> *I like it when you...*
> *I appreciate it when you...*

Be as specific as you can:

> *I like it when you help me with my Math.*
> *I like your creativity in Art.*

2. Pass out a blank 8.5 x 11 sheet of paper to each student and a couple of pieces of tape. Have the students tape the sheet of paper to their backs. Tell them to roam around the room writing validations on each other's backs. It is important to stress that they write something on each person's backs.

3. ***Caution:*** Mention that no one is to write anything but validations. If anyone sees a single negative remark on one of the sheets, this is to be reported immediately, and all the sheets will be collected. This usually prevents problems.

4. After they finish writing, give them time to remove and read their own sheet.

5. Take a few minutes to process the activity with them:
    a. How does it feel to be validated?
    b. What did you learn that others appreciate about you?
    c. How does being validated increase self-confidence?
    d. How did it feel to validate others?
    e. How can we continue to show our appreciation for others?

Source: Skills for adolescence. (1985). Columbus, OH: The Quest National Center.

Who's in the Bag?

Prevention:	Self-esteem
Curricular Area:	Social Studies
Grades:	6-8
Size:	Full class
Time:	60 minutes
Purpose:	To help students better understand and appreciate their uniqueness.

Outcomes: *The students will be able to:*
1. Select items that represent their personal characteristics;
2. Deduce which student is represented by the contents in the bag;
3. Discuss the meaning of items with the group and recognize their own uniqueness.

Materials:
1. Brown bags or other such opaque paper containers
2. Items from home

Procedures:
1. Ask each student to bring an unmarked bag from home containing five items that say something about who the student is. The teacher may want to do this himself/herself to demonstrate the process, serve as a positive model and allay any fears of the children about the kinds of things to bring.
2. The teacher collects the bags and empties one bag at a time before the class.
3. The students try to guess the identity of the owner by discussing the contents of the bag with each other.
4. Before the bag owner identifies himself/herself, have each member of the class point to who he/she thinks is the owner of the bag. Do this on the count of three and as a group, not individually.
5. Spend some time at the end of the guessing in discussing:
   a. What were you saying about yourself by the items you brought?
   b. How did you feel when the contents of your bag were revealed?
   c. What did you learn about yourself? About others?

Source: Canfield, J., & Wells, H.C. (1976). *100 ways to enhance self-concept in the classroom.* Englewood Cliffs, NJ: Prentice-Hall, Inc.

Family Ties

Prevention:	Security, Self-worth
Curricular Areas:	Language Arts, Social Studies
Grades:	6–8
Size:	Full class
Time:	30–40 minutes
Purpose:	To enhance the students' understanding of the role that the family plays in meeting the needs of its members and building security within its members.
Outcomes:	*The students will be able to:*

1. Identify words or phrases that describe what a family is;
2. Identify ways a family meets the needs of its members;
3. Recognize how families have changed over the past two generations;
4. Recognize how families differ in various parts of the world.

Materials:
1. Chalkboard or chart
2. Handout: "Families Past and Present" (see page 73)

Procedures:
1. Introduce the following two activities on families by beginning to define what families are:
2. Write the word family on a chalkboard or chart. Ask the students to brainstorm words or phrases that describe what a family is and record their suggestions. Some examples include:

> *Group of people*   *Same home*
> *Relatives*   *Taking care of each other*
> *Parents raising kids*   *Brothers-sisters*
> *Grandparents*

3. Ask the class to develop a definition of family using their words and phrases. Write the word Needs on the board or chart and ask the class to brainstorm many different needs that family members have and that are met by the family. Some examples include:

> *Rules for behavior*   *Food, shelter, clothing*
> *Love*   *Values*
> *Care*   *Spiritual beliefs*
> *Traditions*

4. Ask the students to share similarities or differences that they have observed about families from cultures different from their own. Record the information about families of other cultures on the board or chart.
5. Distribute the handout, "Families Past and Present." Ask students to complete it at home and bring it to the next session.

Source: Skills for adolescence. (1985). The Quest National Center, 6655 Sharon Woods Blvd., Columbus, Ohio 43229.

Family Communication

Prevention:	Security, Self-worth
Curricular Areas:	Social Studies, Language Arts
Grades:	6–8
Size:	Full class
Time:	90–120 minutes
Purpose:	To help students recognize the benefits of positive and supportive family communication.
Outcomes:	*The students will be able to:*

1. Discuss their own families' unique qualities, values, traditions and the roles fulfilled by members;
2. Compare and contrast families in other cultures;
3. Recognize positive supportive communication in a family as well as negative and unsupportive communication;
4. Role play both types of communication;
5. Generate ways to improve communication within a family.

Materials: Completed handout "Families Past and Present" (see page 73)

Procedures:

1. Allow time for the students to share and discuss information gathered at home on their handouts. Some suggested questions for discussion:
   a. What did you learn about the childhood experiences of your parents or grandparents?
   b. What similarities did you notice between their experiences and your own? What differences?
   c. What traditions or values are present in your family today that were also important to your grandparents and parents?
   d. Talk about the family roles played by different members of the family.
   e. How do the roles that different family members play help things go smoothly?
2. Ask the students what they know about families in other cultures or countries. What was similar to their own family? What was different?
3. Explain that the interviews allowed them to communicate in some depth with family members on a one-to-one basis. As a group, however, families tend to have different "styles" of communication. Some families are positive and supportive while others are negative and unsupportive. Some listen well to each other and some don't. Most families combine these two general styles of communication. Support from family is important for good feelings and healthy development.

4. Briefly describe two families: The **Blockers** and the **Lovelys**. The Blockers are extreme in non-effective communication—much shouting and no listening. The Lovelys are just as extreme in that everyone talks in soft voices and smiles all the time—never a conflict or unpleasant word.

5. Break the students up into groups of four or five to become a family. Give them a possible situation from the list below and ask them to take parts as a mother, father or child. Have them make up a skit showing the Blocker and Lovely styles of communication:

   - The family preparing for out-of-town guests
   - The family at dinner
   - The family on vacation
   - The family in the morning

6. After the skit demonstrations, discuss the problems of both styles of communication as well as any positive aspects of the communication shown in the skits. Discuss how the different styles of communication used by members of the family affect each other. Discuss ways that communication can be improved within a family.

Families Past and Present

Interview Form

1. Ask your father or mother or both to describe what their family was like when they were your age:

2. Ask your father or mother to tell you what they know about the childhood family experiences of one of their parents (or grandparents).

3. What are the roles these people play in your family?

    Mother: _____

    Father: _____

    Brother(s): _____

    Sister(s): _____

    Grandparent(s): _____

    You: _____

PACE

Prevention:	Control, Security, Self-worth
Curricular Areas:	Social Studies, Language Arts
Grades:	6-8
Size:	Full class or groups
Time:	60–180 minutes, several class periods
Purpose:	To help the students realize that evaluating alternatives and their consequences is helpful in making decisions and solving problems.

Outcomes: *The students will be able to:*

1. List decisions they have made during the previous day and identify the consequences of those decisions;
2. Identify problems that students their age have;
3. Name the steps of the PACE model;
4. Explain the steps of the PACE model;
5. Illustrate the use of the steps of the PACE model through role playing a problem situation;
6. Create their own decision-making model and teach it to other students.

Materials: None

Procedure:

1. Ask the students to write down at least 10 decisions (no matter how small) they have made in the last day (24 hours). Ask them also to record the consequences of their decisions and whether the consequences were negative or positive for them.

   For example:

Decisions	**Consequences**	**- or +**
a. Selected clothes for school	were uncomfortable	-
	received compliments	+
b. Watched TV instead of studying for a test	flunked the test	-
	enjoyed the show	+

2. Discuss how decisions sometimes have negative and positive consequences. When we weigh the negative and positive consequences ahead of time, we can make a better decision.
3. Now ask the students to list 10 problems that they feel students their age have to cope with. They may be school-, friend-, or home-related problems.
4. Teach the steps of the PACE decision-making model:

P	**Problem**	Identify the problem specifically
A	**Alternatives**	Explore all the possible alternatives and the consequences of each

C	**Choose** a plan of action	Decide on one of the alternatives
E	**Evaluate** the results of your decision	Was it a good decision? Why or why not?

5. Break into small groups (4–5) and, using a problem identified by the students, apply the model and ask them to prepare a role play (skit showing the steps of the model being used to make a decision).

6. After the skit presentations, discuss how effective or helpful the model was in making decisions. An excellent follow-up is to give students time in small groups to design their own decision-making model and teach it to the class in a creative way. They must be sure to include the basic steps of any decision-making model. If equipment is available, videotaping them teaching their model is very effective.

Planning a *Real* School Project

Prevention:	Control, Security, Self-worth
Curricular Area:	Any Content Area
Grades:	6–8
Size:	Full class
Time:	May be accomplished over several months
Purpose:	To help the students experience making decisions, working with peers and contributing to the school through planning a service project.
Outcomes:	*The students will be able to:*

1. Generate ideas for service projects;
2. Make a group decision selecting a project;
3. Plan the necessary steps to accomplish the project;
4. Implement the steps to the completion of the project.

Materials: None

Procedures:

1. Present the idea of undertaking a class project that will benefit the school, other students, and make a lasting, tangible contribution to the school. Explain that this will be an opportunity to work together as a group, make decisions, and feel a sense of accomplishment.
2. The students should generate their own ideas, select one project as a group, plan the timeline and steps, identify materials and resources, decide tasks and assign responsibilities.
3. Time will have to be set aside weekly for planning, and the project selected will need approval by the administration. Some projects that have been implemented in other schools are:
   a. building an obstacle course
   b. creating and performing a puppet show
   c. raising money to purchase new library books
   d. planting and harvesting a garden
   e. painting a mural in the school
   f. improving the landscaping of the campus
4. Be sure to allow time for evaluation during and at the completion of the projects. It will be helpful for students to assess the following:
   a. how they feel about the project,
   b. how the group is cooperating,
   c. how students are cooperating within the group, and
   d. what they have learned about themselves and others.

Section 4

Stress Reducing Activities

Relaxation Exercises and Guided Imagery

Prevention:	Stress
Curricular Area:	Physical Education, regular classroom
Grades:	K–8
Size:	Full class
Time:	10–20 minutes
Purpose:	To diminish the effects of fears and stress.

Outcomes: *The students will be able to:*
1. Reduce the physical tension in their bodies;
2. Use their imaginations creatively to help manage stress;
3. Reduce tension due to fears and stress.

Materials:
1. Relaxation scripts (see following pages)
2. Tape recorder with soft music (optional)

Procedures:
1. Relaxation exercises designed especially for children can help them to become aware of the feelings of body tension and provide skills to reduce it. Reducing muscle tension seems to help reduce anxiety as well. Using guided imagery and pleasant fantasies can also help reduce anxiety as well as stimulate children's imaginations and enrich the learning process in children.
2. Relaxation training and guided imagery can be conducted in a regular classroom or physical education class, with a large or a small group. Once children develop the skills, they can use them to relax in many different settings without an instructor. Incorporating imagery or fantasy with relaxation exercises serves to maintain the child's interest.
3. These general guidelines should be followed:
   a. Use a soft, even voice.
   b. Prepare students to enter a relaxed state as well as leave the relaxed state.
   c. Adjust time according to age level: K–3: 10 to 15 minutes per session; 4–8: 15 to 20 minutes per session.
   d. Two to three sessions per week will help to establish the exercises with the students.
   e. Background music can enhance the effects of the exercises.

Five-Minute Stress Relievers

Prevention:	Stress
Curricular Area:	At any opportune time during the day
Grades:	K–4
Size:	Full class
Time:	5 minutes

Young children experience varying degrees of tension that may be the result of feelings of fear or anxiety in their everyday life. Academic and social development can be hampered by general worry throughout the day as well as a temporary "uptight" feeling. Often the adults in a child's life (parents, teachers, etc.) can control the situations or conditions a child experiences and, whenever possible, should find ways of altering the situation to make it less stressful for the child.

Teachers can use quieting tricks and exercises to reduce tension and stress in the classroom as well as teach their students something they can utilize anytime they feel the tension begin to build. The idea is to put these quieting tricks into action before stress, tension or anxiety are at a peak.

1. **"Think of Something Quiet."** Raise your voice just slightly and say, *"Look at me. I want you all to think of something very very quiet. Don't tell me what it is, but I'm going to be able to look at each of your faces and I'll be able to tell if you're thinking of something quiet."* The children will respond instantly as you search their faces for the relaxed mental state and the whole emotional tenor of the room will change.

2. **"Mr. Nobody."** You can also reduce stress with humor. Open the classroom door and say, *"Oh, hello, Mr. Nobody. Come in."* This grabs the children's attention because they can see no one is there. Place a chair for Mr. Nobody and invite him to be seated. One by one, the children join in fantasy, and this brief dose of whimsy makes for a calmer approach to the remainder of the day.

3. **"Hand Squeeze."** Don't take hand-holding or hand-touching for granted. It's a way of enhancing interpersonal communication skills. Ask everyone to form a circle (sitting or standing) and to hold hands. You begin by gently squeezing the hand of the child to your right, then relaxing your grip. Be sure to reinforce that they should "touch gently." That child then squeezes the hand of the child to his/her right, then relaxes his/her grip. Continue around the circle. Do a few group squeezes in unison

and say, "Hold. Squeeze. Hold. Squeeze," for whatever length of time seems appropriate.

4. The following is a quieting activity that can be done in 5 minutes after students finish outdoor play, before beginning a test or any other time when the students may need a quieting activity. This can be done as they sit in a chair or at a desk. The teacher sits in front of the students and, with a calming voice tone, tells the story and demonstrates the motions.

"Canoe Trip Down a Jungle River"

"We are going to take a canoe trip down a quiet jungle river. Let's begin paddling."
(Paddle to the left and right)

"Look to the left at the beautifully colored parrots perched on the tree branches."
(Look left)

"Look to the right at the amusing monkeys playing in the trees."
(Look right)

"We're getting hungry. Let's paddle under that tree ahead to pick some of the fruit that is hanging from those low branches. Pick some fruit with both hands. Take a bite of the sweet, juicy fruit. It tastes delicious. Take another bite. Chew."
(Paddle, reach up with each hand, bite and chew)

"Let's paddle on. There are some alligators on the bank to the left of us. Lets paddle more quickly. They're not interested in us. We can slow down."
(Paddle left and right slowly and more quickly)

"Oh, our boat has a leak. Get the bucket and start bailing water out of the boat. Take a piece of gum out of your mouth and push it down into the hole until we can fix it properly."
(Lean over and bail water over each shoulder. Lean over— push the gum in the hole)

"We're getting tired. Let's stop for a rest under that big clump of trees ahead. Lay your paddle down. Its so cool under these trees. Close your eyes. Listen to the birds calling each other. Feel the coolness of the air. Listen to the water slapping lightly against the boat. Breathe deeply and slowly. Open your eyes. We're ready to go on." (to the next activity, test or whatever)
(Hands free in lap, breathe slowly and deeply three times)

Source: *Think of Something Quiet* by Clare Cherry.

Relaxation Script

Prevention:	Stress
Curricular Area:	At any opportune time during the day
Grades:	K–4
Size:	Full class
Time:	10–15 minutes

Hands and Arms

Pretend you have a whole lemon in your left hand. Now squeeze it hard. Try to squeeze all the juice out. Feel the tightness in your hand and arm as you squeeze. Now drop the lemon. Notice how your muscles feel when they are relaxed. Take another lemon and squeeze it. Try to squeeze this one harder than you did the first one. That's right. Real hard. Now drop your lemon and relax. See how much better your hand and arm feel when they are relaxed. Once again, take a lemon in your left hand and squeeze all the juice out. Don't leave a single drop. Squeeze hard. Good. Now relax and let the lemon fall from your hand. *[Repeat process for the right hand and arm.]*

Arms and Shoulders

Pretend you are a furry, lazy cat. You want to stretch. Stretch your arms out in front of you. Place them up high over your head, way back. Feel the pull in your shoulders. Stretch higher. Now just let your arms drop back to your side. Okay, kittens, let's stretch again. Stretch your arms out in front of you. Raise them over your head. Put them back, way back. Pull hard. Now let them drop quickly. Good. Notice how your shoulders feel more relaxed. This time let's have a great big stretch. Try to touch the ceiling. Stretch your arms way out in front of you. Raise them way up high over your head. Push them way, way back. Notice the tension and pull in your arms and shoulders. Hold tight, now. Great. Let them drop very quickly and feel how good it is to be relaxed. It feels good and warm and lazy.

Shoulder and Neck

Now pretend you are a turtle. You're sitting out on a rock by a lake or a peaceful pond, just relaxing in the warm sun. It feels nice and warm and safe here. Oh-oh! You sense danger. Pull your head into your house. Try to pull your shoulders up to your ears and push your head down into your shoulders. Hold in tight. It isn't easy to be a turtle in a shell. The danger is past now. You can come out into the warm sunshine, and, once again, you can relax and feel the warm sunshine. Watch out now! More danger. Hurry, pull your head back into your house and hold it tight. You have to be closed in tight to protect yourself. Okay, you can relax now. Bring your head out and let your shoulders relax. Notice how much better it feels to be relaxed than to be all tight. One more time, now. Danger! Pull your head in. Push your shoulders way up to your ears and hold tight. Don't let even a tiny piece of your head show outside your shell. Hold it. Feel the tenseness in your neck and shoulders. Okay. You can come out now. It's safe again. Relax and feel comfortable in your safety. There's no more danger. Nothing to worry about. Nothing to be afraid of. You feel good.

Jaw

You have a giant jawbreaker bubble gum in your mouth. It's very hard to chew. Bite down on it. Hard! Let your neck muscles help you. Now relax. Just let your jaw hang loose. Notice how good it feels just to let your jaw drop. Okay, let's tackle that jawbreaker again now. Bite down. Hard! Try to squeeze it out between your teeth. That's good. You're really tearing that gum up. Now relax again. Just let your jaw drop off your face. It feels so good just to let go and not have to fight that bubble gum. Okay, one more time. We're really going to tear it up this time. Bite down. Hard as you can. Harder. Oh, you're really working hard. Good. Now relax. Try to relax your whole body. You've beaten the bubble gum. Let yourself go as loose as you can.

Stomach

This time imagine that you want to squeeze through a narrow fence and the boards have splinters on them. You'll have to make yourself very skinny if you're going to make it through. Suck your stomach in. Try to squeeze it up against your backbone. Try to be as skinny as you can. You've got to get through. Now relax. You don't have to be skinny now. Just relax and feel your stomach being warm and lose. Okay, lets try to get through that fence now. Squeeze up your stomach. Make it touch your back bone. Get it real small and tight. Get as skinny as you can. Hold tight, now. You've got to squeeze through. You got through that skinny little fence and no splinters. You can relax now. Settle back and let your stomach come back out where it belongs. You can feel really good now. You've done fine.

Legs and Feet

Now pretend that you are standing barefoot in a big, fat mud puddle. Squish your toes down deep into the mud. Try to get your feet down to the bottom of the mud puddle. You'll probably need your legs to help you push. Push down, spread your toes apart, and feel the mud squish up between your toes. Now step out of the mud puddle. Relax your feet. Let your toes go loose and feel how nice that is. It feels good to be relaxed. Back into the mud puddle. Squish you toes down. Let your leg muscles help push your feet down. Push your feet. Hard. Try to squeeze that mud puddle dry. Okay. Come back out now. Relax your feet, relax your legs, relax your toes. It feels so good to be relaxed. No tenseness anywhere. You feel kind of warm and tingly.

Conclusion

Stay as relaxed as you can. Let your whole body go limp and feel all your muscles relaxed. In a few minutes I will ask you to open your eyes, and that will be the end of this session. As you go through the day, remember how good it feels to be relaxed. Sometimes you have to make yourself tighter before you can be relaxed, just as we did in these exercises. Practice these exercises every day to get more and more relaxed. A good time to practice is at night, after you have gone to bed and the lights are out and you won't be disturbed. It will help you get to sleep. Then, when you are a really good relaxer, you can help yourself relax here at school. Just remember the elephant, or the jaw breaker, or the mud puddle, and you can do these exercises and nobody will know. You've worked hard today, and it feels good to work hard. Very slowly, now, open your eyes and wiggle your muscles around a little. Very good. You've done a good job. You're going to be a super relaxer.

Source: Koeppen, A. S. (1974). Relaxation training for children. *Elementary School Guidance and Counseling,* October issue.

Relaxation Scripts

Prevention:	Stress
Curricular Area:	At any opportune time during the day
Grades:	5–8
Size:	Full class
Time:	10–15 minutes

Script #1

Settle back in your seat (or on the floor) and get comfortable in your space. Squint your eyes and tense your face as if you were on a sandy beach looking into the bright sun. Now feel the cool breeze blowing and relax every muscle in your face. Close your eyelids and relax your mouth.

Pull your shoulders up toward your ears. Imagine a heavy brick on each shoulder and how much exertion it takes to lift your shoulders. Now imagine the bricks falling away and your shoulders are free, loose and very relaxed.

Now make a fist as tight as you can. Flex every muscle in your arm. Command all your strength and power to go into those arm muscles. Now relax your arms, wrists and hands. Allow your arms to go limp, to droop at your side or rest in your lap.

Pull your stomach in as tight as you can. Imagine you are trying to squeeze through a very narrow crack in a rock wall. Tighten those stomach muscles. You made it through. Now you can relax all those muscles in your stomach and take a deep breath, filling your diaphragm and stomach with air.

Try to press your ankles together as tightly as you can. Hold that position, pressing them closer and closer together. Now let your legs fall apart loosely. Let them hang heavy from your chair (or sink heavily into the floor). Press your feet against the floor as hard as you can (bend knees to do this if lying on the floor). Try to push a hole right through the floor. Now the floor has dropped out from under you feet. Let them dangle loosely.

Now we will take three slow, deep breaths, counting to 10 with each one, inhaling on 1–5 and exhaling on 6–10. Fill your stomach, diaphragm and lungs with oxygen completely filling up until there is no space left—and then exhale all the stale air slowly.

Script #2

Close your eyes. Tense your whole body for a moment as you take a deep breath. Hold the tension and hold your breath for a moment...Now let go and exhale, letting your whole body relax... Let go and relax even more. Your whole body can let go and feel really peaceful and comfortable.

[Pause 10 seconds]

Picture all of the tension in your head and face coming together into a big knot in your forehead. Study the knot for a moment; concentrate on it...Now let it dissolve and melt, letting all the tension go from your head and face.

[Pause]

Now imagine all the tension in your throat coming together in a knot. In this knot are the unspoken needs and feelings you have held back, all of the feelings you've swallowed. Put all of those tensions in the knot, then let it untie...The knot melts and dissolves, taking all of the tension with it.

[Pause]

Now imagine all of the tension in your chest in a big knot around your heart. Feel how tense the knot is...then let the knot untie... melting and dissolving all the tension in your chest.

[Pause]

Now imagine all the tension in your stomach in a big knot down there. Feel it, see it, understand it...Now let the knot untie...letting all your tension melt and dissolve.

[Pause]

Imagine that a big knot holds all of the rest of the tension in your body. Study the knot for a moment, feel it, understand it...Now let it untie...Let it melt and dissolve...All of the tension drains from your body.

[Pause]

Now imagine that all the tensions between you and other people around you are a bunch of knots. Tensions build up around us, making knots between us and others. Feel and understand the knots...Now let them untie, dissolving and melting all of the tension from between you. Then feel and enjoy the relaxation...no knots between you.

[Pause]

And when you are ready, slowly open your eyes, stretch, and get up feeling rested and alert.

Script #3

Everybody has many different feelings during the day. Things may make us angry, scared, hurt, happy, or excited. Sometimes if you let yourself feel them at the the time, they will dissolve and won't store up. But a lot of times we forget to let ourselves feel our feelings, so they get stored up inside us. Then they come out in ways that sometimes hurt us and people around us. We'll touch bases with a few different feelings that all of us feel. Take a moment to get your body as relaxed as you can. Close your eyes and let your mind relax.

[Pause 5–10 seconds]

Picture a thing or two that you may have felt angry about recently...See it...Feel it in your body...Give yourself total permission to feel it...then relax and let it go.

[Pause 10 seconds]

Now picture a time or two when you've felt hurt...when your feelings have been hurt...or when you've felt rejected....Just be with the feelings for a moment...Let yourself feel them...then let them go and relax.

[Pause]

Let yourself get in touch with times you've felt scared recently... Picture the situation in your mind...Feel it in your body...Just let yourself feel scared for a moment...Then relax and let the feelings go.

[Pause]

When you have feelings going on inside you, take a moment to feel them deeply. This will keep you from building them up and carrying them around with you. Take a moment now to feel any other feelings that we haven't touched.

[Pause]

Then when you are ready, bring yourself back to alertness and give your body a good stretch.

Source of scripts 2 & 3: Hendricks, G. (1979). *The family centering book.* Englewood Cliffs, NJ: Prentice-Hall.

Section 5

High Risk Student Activities

ESL Activities

High Risk:	Security, Control, Self-worth
Curricular Area:	ESL
Grades:	K–8
Size:	Individual
Time:	Varies
Purpose:	To help allay the fears of non-English speaking students in the environment of the school and in the community.
Outcomes:	*The students will be able to:*
	1. Relax and be calm in the school environment;
	2. Begin to enter into the life of the school;
	3. Begin to construct positive social relationships with peers.
Materials:	See individual activities below.
Procedures:	*The Non-English Speaking Child:* One of the most frightening experiences for children is to enroll at a new school in which the language of instruction is unfamiliar to the student. If the child's teachers do not know the language of the child, it can be doubly stressful for the child and a source of frustration for the adults as well since language cannot be used as a mediator between the child and his/her fears. The child placed in such a seemingly hostile environment will most likely feel insecure, will probably experience a loss of control over his/her life, and will possibly lose a substantial portion of his/her sense of self-worth since he/she will not be able to function at the level that he/she had attained in the past. The following procedures may be able to alleviate some of the deleterious effects of this unpleasant experience:

1. *Security Blankets:* Find out from the parents what conveys the notion of warmth and acceptance within the culture of the child. It may be physical contact (hugs), facial expressions, food, or any number of culturally appropriate behaviors or objects. Whatever it is, make sure that you are aware of it and can demonstrate it to the child.
2. *Peer Power:* If there are other students within the class or within the school who speak the language of the child, plan to pair up the new child with the veteran immediately. The peer will serve as an ally for the affected child and will increase his/her sense of security. Even if there is no one who speaks the language of the child, select an especially friendly and outgoing student to be the newcomer's special "buddy."
   a. Have the peer helper show the newcomer the layout of the school, explain the school schedule and routines, and act as an interpreter between school personnel and the child, if he/she speaks the child's language.

b. It is a good idea to develop a peer helper program to train a cadre of students to act as peer facilitators. Have the helpers brainstorm ideas about what it was like to be new and what kinds of things they needed when they were newcomers with little or no language skills. Make sure that they understand that they are to help acclimate the new students so that they can begin to do things for themselves and that they are not expected to do everything for the newcomers on a sustained basis.

3. *Pictures as Words:* If there is no one in the school who speaks the language of the child, draw pictures to communicate with the child. Draw a clock with pictures of what happens during the day at certain times, such as children playing when it is time for recess, etc.

4. *Physical Activity:* Make sure that all ESL students are heavily involved during those times in the school day when physical exercise is taken. Never remove them from PE or recess, even for extra language study. Physical activity can serve to mitigate the effects of stress, is an optimum time for new ESL students to compete on even terms with their peers (thus restoring self-worth), can be an excellent chance for students to bond with their peers, and is an opportunity for "informal" language learning to take place.

5. *Welcome Ceremony:* Set aside some time for the new child to meet his/her classmates. Have a group of students act as a welcoming committee and plan a mini-party in which food and small gifts are shared with the newcomer to make him/her feel as if he/she were a valued addition to the group. Introduce the child to the class and have each student introduce him or herself to the newcomer and greet him/her with a warm "Welcome!"

6. *Community Orientation:* Arrange for a student or group of students to take the newcomer on a tour of the community. A visit to the local market, if in a traditional culture community, would be an excellent place to begin as markets are often intimidating, yet are the centers of life in many areas. Have the students show the child what things are available, how the system of economic transactions functions (i.e., bargaining, etc.), and how to get around in the community.

7. *Parent Involvement:* Make sure that the parents of the new child are thoroughly oriented to the policies and routines of the school so that the child may use them as a resource after the school day is over.

Personal Crisis Management

High Risk:	Security, Control
Curricular Area:	Counseling
Grades:	K–8
Size:	Individual, group, full class
Time:	Varies
Purpose:	To help children express feelings and thoughts related to a personal crisis event and develop coping strategies that may be helpful in coping with a crisis situation.

Outcomes: *The students will be able to:*
1. Define the meaning of crisis;
2. Identify feelings and thoughts related to experiencing a crisis;
3. Discuss actions that would be helpful to take in a crisis situation;
4. Generate steps that can be taken when facing a personal crisis.

Materials:
1. chalkboard or
2. chart and marker

Procedures: The occurrence of a personal or situational crisis in an elementary child's life may impair normal emotional functioning. These crises could include death of a relative or friend, divorce or separation, neglect, abuse, parent's loss of a job, moving abroad, experiencing a different culture for the first time, illness or accident.

1. ***Individual:*** Listening to a student who is experiencing a personal crisis and creating an accepting, nonjudgmental atmosphere helps the student unlock feelings and express thoughts, anxieties or fears related to the situation. Rather than give advice, the teacher can serve as a mirror reflecting back to the child the feelings and thoughts expressed. The child may not wish to communicate verbally. Just being with someone who cares about him/her may help the child feel more secure. Playing games, drawing or reading a book together are other ways of expressing care and concern for the child.

2. ***Small Group:*** Small group discussions led by a teacher may be a mode of support for children experiencing a common crisis or similar situation. Participants in a group learn that they are reacting naturally which can reduce their feelings of loneliness and of being different. For example, children who share the common experience of their parents' divorce may express similar feelings, recognize common situations, hear other's coping strategies and find support and help through the phases of adjustment. Goals of a small discussion group should include helping the children express feelings, understanding what happened and why, and deciding what action can be taken to cope with the crisis.

3. ***Classroom Guidance:*** A classroom guidance approach can be a means of helping children who are experiencing a personal crisis to develop adaptive coping behaviors as well as provide each of the students with an opportunity to develop coping skills before a crisis event occurs. The following classroom guidance approach can be divided into several lessons:

    a. Using a brainstorming technique, lead the children toward formulation of a composite definition of the word "crisis." Fill the chalkboard or a chart with as many crisis events that can happen to a student as they can generate.

    b. Ask the students to select a crisis event that happened to them, or someone they know, and draw a picture about the event and/or write a story about it. Younger children may choose drawing and older children may prefer to write. Allow enough time for the children to thoroughly develop their writing or drawing.

    c. Encourage the students to share their writing or drawing with the class including any details of the event or feelings elicited by the event that they wish to share.

    d. Use the brainstorming technique again to identify various feelings experienced during a personal crisis. Ask the students to also brainstorm some of the things they think about during a crisis event.

    e. It is important to include an action phase in the classroom guidance approach. Lead the students to a discussion of action strategies using the following questions:

        > *What did you do that helped you in a time of crisis?*
        > *Who might help you in a time of crisis?*
        > *What steps might you take to help yourself if you are facing a crisis event?*

    f. As a means of culminating the classroom guidance approach, the teacher should formulate a summarization of the main points of the lessons and allow the students to summarize what they have learned about handling a crisis situation in their life.

4. Taking time to structure a small group discussion or classroom guidance approach will help a teacher recognize some of the personal struggles of their students. It may also help identify students and families who may benefit from more professional help and with whom the teacher may want to remain in closer communication. Schools need to recognize the effects personal crisis have on students and learning and perhaps develop policies for dealing with children in crisis.

Collective Crisis Management

High Risk:	Security, Control
Curricular Area:	Counseling
Grades:	K–8
Size:	Full class
Time:	Varies
Purpose:	To help students cope with the stress and fear due to collective crises which may occur in or around the school.

Outcomes: *The students will be able to:*
1. Express and accept their fears;
2. Gain a realistic sense of security in relation to a crisis;
3. Remain reasonably in control in relation to a crisis.

Materials: The booklet, *Managing Children During a Crisis*, U.S. Department of State, February, 1986.

Procedures:
1. *Guidelines for Adult Behavior:* Collective crises are rare (but, unfortunately, real) occurrences that affect groups of people, such as a class, a school or an entire community, rather than individuals or isolated families. These crises include accidents, kidnappings, bomb scares and bombings, coups, insurrections, riots and acts of terror. Although the incidence of such crises is low, it is best for teachers, counselors and administrators to be prepared for such eventualities and to be aware of certain generally accepted guidelines for dealing with a collective crisis.

   In the case of a crisis, school personnel should:
   a Be in contact with the parents of the children involved as soon as possible. A free flow of information will serve to calm the fears of both groups and will add to the children's feelings of security;
   b. Not avoid discussion of the incident. To feel fear after a dangerous incident is natural. Children (and adults) need an outlet for their feelings and fears. To ignore the incident will make the children feel that there is something wrong with them for feeling as they do;
   c. Remain calm. Children will look toward adults and adult behavior for security in times of crisis. Panicky adults will only lead to loss of control on the part of the children. Be reassuring and comforting, with liberal use of physical contact;

   d. Be honest and forthright with children. Give supportive information that will build up trust between you and the child. It is better to say, "I don't know" than to deliberately make up something which will later prove false;
   e. Mobilize the child's own resources. Encourage children to help each other, to talk, sing, play games or whatever else is appropriate for lifting spirits and distraction. Allow students to help with chores, clean up, distribute food, etc.—all things that will permit them to feel in control.
2. ***Activities During a Threat Period:*** During periods of stress due to social, political or environmental factors, teachers, counselors and administrators should discuss the following:
   a   Roles and tasks of each staff member during the crisis;
   b. Communication/information systems, such as radios, telephone networks, emergency channels, etc.
   c. First aid procedures;
   d   Stress management and relaxation techniques for periods of confinement;
   e. Adult fears and communicating to children about fears and other emotions;
   f. Preparation for post-violent incident classroom activities;
   g. Procedures for evacuation from school.
3. ***Classroom Activities Following a Crisis:***
   a   Unfinished sentences:

> *During the _____ , I was scared when _____.*
> *When I heard that _____, I felt _____.*
> *I still think about _____.*
> *When I (see, pass by, hear) _____. I think about _____ and I feel _____.*

   b. Drawings to accompany sentences

> *Pictures of what happened*
> *People it happened to*
> *Yourself [the child] at the time*
> *Composite picture of event on a large board or mural*

   c. Re-enacting the event with children (or puppets, dolls, etc.) taking the roles

   d   Teacher-led discussions

> *Who did what and why*
> *What they might have done*
> *What we know now that we didn't know then*

   e. Poems, stories, songs, letters, assemblies, discussions and drills dealing with the event or similar events

Source: U.S. Dept. of State. (1986). *Managing children during a crisis.* Washington, DC: Author.

Systematic Desensitization

High Risk:	Control
Curricular Area:	Counseling
Grades:	K–8
Size:	Individual
Time:	30–45 minutes per session
Purpose:	To help students deal with their unreasonable fears.
Outcomes:	*The students will be able to:*

The students will be able to:
1. Relax when faced with feelings of fear;
2. Control their fears so as to be able to enter into the activities of the school.

Materials: A hierarchy of situations related to the client's fear.

Procedures: Systematic desensitization is a technique used by mental health professionals to treat clients who experience unreasonable emotional reactions, such as intense fear, when confronted with situations which are not dangerous in and of themselves. This technique is especially useful in the treatment of common phobias, such as the fear of heights, claustrophobia, and the fear most commonly found in students, school phobia.

The technique focuses on pairing **relaxation behavior** with **mental images** of fear-inducing stimuli organized in a graduated hierarchy. In other words, the client is told to imagine things which more and more approximate the phobic situation that he fears in real life while at the same time relaxing. By mixing fear producing situations with relaxing behavior, the technique gradually breaks down the association of the feared object with the fear response because a person cannot be tense (a physiological response to fear) and relaxed at the same time.

1. The first step is to construct a hierarchy of images which are related to the client's fear or phobia. The hierarchy should begin with something which is only remotely connected to the fearful situation and then, in gradual approximations, the images should become more and more similar to the actual fear. For example, if a student has a fear of going to school, one could start with something relatively benign, such as getting up in the morning. Then, one could progress gradually through all the steps that lead to going to school itself. Finally, one can arrive at the school.
2. The second step is to teach the client relaxing behavior (see *Relaxation Scripts*, pp. 85–87). The relaxing behavior must be taught to the client before beginning to introduce the hierarchy so that relaxation can be paired with the mental images.

3. What follows is a script of a session of systematic desensitization with a ten-year-old who, because of his father's frequent job
changes, must change schools often. Unfortunately, he has a
fear of meeting new people which has generalized to a case of
school phobia. Three different levels of the hierarchy will be
presented:

Counselor: "Last time we talked about how you get very
nervous about meeting kids at school. You've explained to me
how you feel scared at the thought of starting a conversation
with someone whom you don't know. You said that your palms
start to sweat, your heart begins to beat faster and you feel
short of breath and uncomfortable. The only way that you have
been able to control this reaction is to avoid the situation and
stay by yourself. You said that it has become so bad that you
don't even want to go to school anymore. Is that about right?"

Student: "That's right."

Counselor: "OK, you also said that despite these feelings, what
you really want is to feel comfortable enough at school with
other students to make friends. We agreed that with your family
moving around so much, and you having to attend different
schools so frequently, it's a real pain not to be able to make
friends comfortably like the other kids. Would you say that
describes how you feel?"

Student: "Yes."

Counselor: "Great. Well, we can work on this problem by using
a procedure with a fancy name--desensitization. By using
desensitization, those situation that make you feel tense and
nervous now will no longer cause you to feel bad. The procedure
has been used very successfully with thousands of people all
over the world to help them reduce their fears of certain
situations. I feel it can work with you too."

To make this work, you will first learn how to relax. After you're
relaxed, I ask you to imagine some things about meeting people,
starting first with things that aren't too frightening, and
gradually thinking about more uncomfortable situations. As we
go along, the relaxation will start to replace the tension and
fear, and some of the things that you might think are stressful
now will no longer seem so bad later. Do you have any questions
about this?"

[The first stage in the hierarchy]

Counselor: "Ok, now that you've learned how to relax, it's time
to try some desensitization. I'm going to ask you to imagine
something. Listen to what I say and try to put a picture of it in

your mind At the same time, just remain relaxed and calm. If you start to feel tense, I want you to raise your pointing finger of your right hand. Let's try that now. "

"Great. All right, now relax as we've just been practicing. Imagine you're lying down in a grassy field on a calm, peaceful day. The sun is warm and there's a gentle breeze blowing on your face. You're just so comfortable lying there that you feel like you're just melting into the grass. The tenseness is leaving your body. You're breathing deeply, and the air feels so fresh and clean. You're calm and relaxed and you feel so good.

"Good. Now imagine you are home and you overhear your parents talking. Your father is telling your mother that he might be transferred to another job and that you might have to move again. You don't know if you will have to move; there is only the possibility that you will have to. Imagine that conversation and keep that image in your mind. Just think about it for a while." *[Wait for 10 seconds]*

"OK, now go back to your relaxing. You didn't raise your finger which means that you didn't feel very tense, right?"

Student: "Right."

Counselor: "Good. Let's do it again. *[Repeat the scene]*

"That's great. You got through that without any trouble. Let's try another.

[Skipping several steps in the hierarchy]

Counselor: "Ok, you've been doing just fine so far. Let's try another one. Now just relax and imagine the next scene that I describe to you. It's the first day at your new school, and you are getting in the car with your mom to go to school. You are opening the door and just getting in, you sit down next to your mom and your mom starts the car. You pull away from the curb..."

Student: *[Raises his finger indicating fear.]*

Counselor: "Ok, just relax. Think of... *[Go back to the relaxation scene]* That's it. Breathe deeply. Feel relaxed?"

"Let's try it again." *[Repeat the same scene. If no fear response, go on to next step in the hierarchy.]*

[Skipping several steps in the hierarchy]

Counselor: "All right. We've gone through a whole list of scenes, and you've managed to stay calm and relaxed through-out the process. Let's give it one more try with a new scene. Now relax again as we practiced."

"You're at school, and the teacher has just let the class out for recess. You're on the playground, and the boys are getting up a game of volleyball. You want to play too, but in order to do so, you have to go over to one of the guys and ask him to let you in on the game. You are walking over to him to talk to him, you are figuring out what you want to say, and he turns around to look at you. Think about that, keep it in your mind, and relax.

Student: *[Raises finger indicating fear]*

Counselor: "OK, relax." *[Bring up the relaxation image again and terminate the session after achieving relaxation.]*

Section 6

Appendices

Appendix 1-A: High Risk Children in Schools

Some children in schools may experience collective or personal disasters in their lives which can lead to problems related to fears and stress. Inviting such children and other adults in their lives to participate in counseling activities is an important strategy for schools to consider in preventing fear-related problems.

Collective disasters might include earthquakes, tornadoes, hurricanes, or a gas explosion that affects a whole neighborhood. In these instances a large portion of a school population or community may be affected. Such crises remind children that they are vulnerable, raise doubts regarding their sense of security, and tend to diminish their sense of control over their own destinies. Although life anywhere is filled with uncertainty, such events can give rise to doubts about their ability to be successful in other areas of their lives and to meet the challenges of daily threats.

Personal disasters, although not necessarily collectively shared, can be just as traumatic for the individual child. Loss of a parent through accident or divorce, bodily injury, and the trauma of a nocturnal break-in or mugging are examples of personal disasters. These may have the same effect on the child as collective disasters. The child who is under stress from such things as changing schools, family strife, school failure, etc. can also be at greater risk than other children.

The counselor, teacher or administrator may wish to target these children and their families for special intervention. The teachers may be uncertain about what to do. Should they go on as usual? Should they talk about it? What do they say if they do talk about it?

Parents, too, may be uncertain what to do. Often in the face of collective or personal disaster, teachers and parents uncertain about how to broach the topic simply return to business as usual, inadvertently sending the message that this is something not to be explored. In such circumstances, the counselor or administrator needs to help teachers, parents and children with the opportunity for some release appropriate to the developmental level of the children.

Suggestions

In cases where collective or personal disasters have occurred teachers should meet with parents first, let them talk out their concerns and fears, then provide them with structured ways they can help children. One suggestion is to have a "sharing time" with the child or children. After the sharing, story time for younger children might help them calm down a bit. One teacher passed out clay during story time. At first, children just kneaded the clay. Later, as their anxiety abated, they began to make things with the clay. Learning how to release the tensions brought on by a crisis situation, then, is the first goal of intervention. Relaxation training, guided imagery, mutual story telling and other techniques might be helpful follow-up activities. With high risk populations, the school personnel will want to deal first with the specific issue at hand—allowing for catharsis—then help the children to re-establish their senses of control, self-worth and security.

Appendix 1-B: Helping the Fearful Child—A Counseling Model

Another level of intervention is helping the child who is already experiencing fear-related problems. The longer fear-related problems persist, the more difficult it is to help the person find ways to overcome his/her fear.

In the following pages, we have outlined a four-phase counseling scheme which follows the model of coping (self-worth, control, security) suggested in this guide. In the first phase, the counselor is concerned with establishing a positive relationship, providing cathartic release, exploring the child's world, and validating the child's fear. This last consideration is most important. The child's fears are real, no matter how mystical, imaginary, or unthreatening they may appear to the observer.

The second phase deals with assessment. This does not necessarily mean testing, but rather getting to know the child from his or her perspective and developing a sense of how the child views the world and his/her place in it. Specifically, the counselor needs to have a clear picture of the child's sense of control, self-worth and security. It may be that a given fear arises out of a specific situation related to personal disaster in which the child feels vulnerable to a specific fear object. In such a situation, the counselor may move on to the third phase, focusing on the child's relationship with fear objects.

On the other hand, the counselor may find that the child's fears are many and varied arising from a lack of security. The child may have little opportunity to act on his/her world, seeing self at the mercy of things in the environment rather than exercising control over the environment. The child may view self as failure-expectant, assuming defeat in the face of life's threats. In such situations, the counselor will proceed into phase three with a different approach.

In phase three, the counselor is concerned with generating and implementing a plan of action to assist the child. For fear specific situations, the counselor and child may implement a number of options, including systematic desensitization, implosive therapy, flooding, cognitive restructuring, cognitive self-control, bibliotherapy relaxation training, etc. Such strategies may be employed individually or in appropriate combination to help the child develop ways to cope with the fear object. If the fear object is a result of a lack of transference of the skills the child already has in coping, or as a result of a particular encounter, such specifically focused interventions have proven successful.

If the child's fears arise from a lack of control, self-worth and/or security, such approaches may help temporarily with the specific situation, but will manifest themselves again in a different situation or with a different fear. In such cases, the counselor may proceed with some of the above strategies, but will also want to help the child develop his/her general sense of control, self-worth and security. Strategies the counselor may wish to employ here might include decision-making and problem solving skills, increasing success experience, interpersonal communication skills training, assertiveness training, etc. The counselor may work directly with the child in individual or group counseling, but should also consider parent and teacher consultation. Consultation might focus on both helping parents and teachers understand childhood fear as well as home and classroom strategies to help the child develop a better sense of control, self-worth and security.

Evaluation

In the last phase, the counselor must assess the impact of the counseling strategies as helping the child deal with fear objects. If the counselor employs a direct strategy, such as systematic desensitization, only to find that one fear object is quickly replaced by another, the counselor may wish to look only at the child's sense of control, self-worth or security to determine if intervention in one or more areas underlying the child's sense of power would be an appropriate focus.

For children who have a positive sense of power, strategies focused on directly reducing the impact of the fear object may take a shorter period of time before results are noted than in the case where the child's sense of power is not strong. While intervention directed at the concepts of control, self-worth and security may take longer to show results, the long term effects of helping children establish a sense of power in their lives will not only help with overcoming fear related problems, but may generalize to other areas of personal functioning.

Model for Counseling the Fearful Child

Stage One: Exploration

This stage allows the child to openly explore feelings, thoughts and behavior regarding self in relation to fear object(s).

Counselor Seeks To:

- Establish an atmosphere of trust and open communication;
- Validate the child's perceptions as real and appropriate at the current level of experiencing and understanding;
- Provide an opportunity for catharsis.

Techniques Utilized:

- Empathic listening and responding
- Appropriate self-disclosure
- Biblio-counseling
- Mutual story telling
- Play, art, storytelling, etc.

Procedural Goal:

- Self-exploration

Stage Two: Assessment

This stage helps the child define the fear in relationship to trauma or disaster and/or current sense of security, self-worth and/or control.

Counselor Seeks To:

- Help the child recognize reactions to traumatic event or disaster;
- Help the child recognize sense of security, self-worth. control;
- Gently guide the child toward recognition of relationship of self with fear object.

Techniques Utilized:

- Continued empathic responding
- Added specificity in responding
- Role play
- Role reversal
- Play, art, storytelling, etc.

Procedural Goal:

- Self-understanding

Stage Three: Intervention

This stage helps the child take appropriate action to deal with fear object(s).

Counselor Seeks To:

- Help the child develop specific strategies in coping with fear object(s) and/or
- Help the child increase sense of security and/or self-worth and/or control.

Techniques Utilized:

- Relaxation training
- Systematic Desensitization
- Guided Imagery
- Interpersonal communication skills training
- Decision making/problem solving skills training
- Life skills training groups
- Creating success experiences
- Biblio-counseling
- Encouragement

Procedural Goal:

- Action directed toward dealing with fear object or increasing sense of security, self-worth and control

Stage Four: Evaluation

This stage helps the child assess current relationship of self to fear objects.

Counselor Seeks To:

- Validate child's ability to cope with fear object(s);
- Validate child's sense of security, self-worth and/or control.

Techniques Utilized:

- Role play
- Role rehearsal
- Role reversal
- Direct observation
- Indirect observation
- Self report

Procedural Goal:

- Evaluation of interaction scheme

Appendix 1-C: Bibliography of Children's Fears

Fear of Change

Coates, Belle. **Mak.** Houghton Mifflin, 1991. **Ages 12 and up.**

In this slowly unfolding, well-written story of an orphaned boy torn between two cultures, the reader gains considerable insight into the feelings, beliefs, and way of life of Native Americans, and in particular, their struggle to retain their culture. Change, Mak finds, is essential, and yet change often pits the old ways against the new.

Fear of the Dark

Bond, Felicia. **Poinsettia Pig and the Firefighters.** Crowell Publishers, 1984. **Ages 4–7.**

Lonely and afraid of the dark in her new room, Poinsettia Pig is comforted when she discovers that the firefighters are awake and keep watch during the night.

Bonsall, Crosby Newell. **Who's Afraid of the Dark?** Harper & Row, 1980. **Ages 3–7.**

A little boy describes his dog's fear of the dark, and his sympathetic friend, recognizing that it is the boy himself who is afraid, gives helpful advice.

Mayer, Mercer. **There's a Nightmare in My Closet.** Dial Press, 1968. **Ages 3–6.**

In an amusing story, a determined young boy decides to take action against his nighttime fears.

Robinson, Deborah. **No Elephants Allowed.** Clarion Books, 1981. **Ages 3–6.**

After receiving well-meant but ineffective help from his family, a little boy deals successfully and in his own way with his nighttime fears.

Schubert, Ingrid and Dieter. **There's a Crocodile Under My Bed.** McGraw Hill, 1981. **Ages 3–6.**

A little girl copes with her bedtime fears by turning the frightening crocodile of her imagination into a gentle, entertaining fantasy, spending an evening with a delightful crocodile whose very job is to reassure her.

Smith, Janice Lee. *The Monster in the Third Dresser Drawer and Other Stories About Adam Joshua.* Harper & Row, 1981. **Ages 5–8.**

In these anecdotal chapters, young Adam Joshua, helped by understanding parents, copes with a move, a new baby sister, and several less dramatic but familiar events.

Stevenson, James. *What's Under My Bed?* Greenwillow Books, 1983. **Ages 4–7.**

Grandpa helps Mary Ann and Louie cope with their nighttime fears by sharing his experiences as a young child.

Willoughby, Elaine Macmann. *Boris and the Monsters.* Houghton Mifflin, 1980. **Ages 4–7.**

A small boy masters his fear of the dark when he moves to protect something more helpless than he is—a frightened puppy.

Zalben, Jane Breskin. *Norton's Nighttime.* William Collins Publishers, 1979. **Ages 2–6.**

A young raccoon named Norton wanders away from his pine tree and cannot find his way home before nightfall. Small children will understand Norton's feelings of fear and insecurity and will laugh with relief as the raccoon discovers his friends.

Fear of Being Lost

Mauser, Pat Rhoads. *How I Found Myself at the Fair.* Atheneum, 1980. **Ages 7–9.**

An only child, used to her mother's close supervision, goes to a state fair with the large, unruly family of a friend and gets lost. After a succession of frightening experiences, Laura uses her head and finds her friends again.

Parenteau, Shirley. *I'll Bet You Thought I Was Lost.* Lothrop, Lee & Shepard Co., 1981. **Ages 5–8.**

A trip to the supermarket with his father becomes a scary adventure when little Sandy gets lost. He tries hard to find something familiar in the people and products he sees, but his panic steadily increases until he finds his father; then the boy is delightfully plucky and brave.

Wittels, Harriet and Griesman, Joan. *Things I Hate.* Behavioral Publications, 1973. **Ages 4–8.**

This story centers on the fear of getting lost and is a good discussion starter.

Fear of Death

Bunting, Anne Evelyn. *The Big Red Barn.* Harcourt, Brace & Jovanovich, 1979. **Ages 4–7.**

In this first-person story, the family barn symbolizes the permanence and security a young boy longs for after the death of his mother and the arrival of his stepmother. When the barn is destroyed, the boy feels doubly threatened. Through the help of his grandfather, he comes to accept the new barn and his new stepmother.

Byars, Betsy Cromer. *Goodbye, Chicken Little.* Harper & Row, 1979. **Ages 9–11.**

In this fast-moving story, a quiet, cautious boy comes to grips with several disturbing events and emotions: grief and guilt over the accidental deaths of close family members; confusion about a friendship; anxiety about his place in an outgoing, often unpredictable family.

Jackson, Jacqueline. *The Taste of Spruce Gum.* Little, Brown & Co., 1966. **Ages 10–13.**

Eleven-year-old Libby is confused by the sudden changes in her life; moving to a new home, and her mother's relationship with another person after the death of her father. The characterizations and human relationships are timeless.

Viorst, Judith. *The Tenth Good Thing About Barney.* Atheneum, 1971. **Ages 4–8.**

With the aid of supportive parents, a young boy deals with the anxieties and grief surrounding the death of his pet cat.

Fear in General

Blume, Judy. *Otherwise Known as Sheila the Great.* E. P. Dutton, 1972. **Ages 9–12.**

Ten-year-old Sheila is afraid of dogs, water, strange noises and imaginary creatures. Rather than admit her fears, she conceals them through constant boasting and lying. With the help of a friend and her parents, she admits her fears and begins to cope with them.

Coles, Alison. EDC Publishing. **Ages 3–7.**
Michael's First Day at School. 1984.
Michael in the Dark. 1984.
Michael and the Sea. 1985.
Mandy and the Hospital. 1985.
Mandy and the Dentist. 1985.

Michael and Mandy are two very normal children and, like every child, they are sometimes afraid of the unknown. These stories show how Michael and many others overcome their fears and enjoy life more fully for having been brave.

Crofford, Emily. *A Matter of Pride.* Carolrhoda Books, 1981. **Ages 8–11.**

A young girl learns what courage can entail through her mother's brave overcoming of her fears in the interest of protecting her family and preserving their few possessions during the Depression.

Heck, Bessie Holland. *Cave-In at Mason's Mine.* Charles Scribners's Sons, 1980. **Ages 8–10.**

A young boy must overcome his fears and practice the new skills his father has taught him in order to save his father's life in this suspenseful adventure.

Tester, Sylvia Root. *Sometimes I'm Afraid.* Children's Press, 1979. **Ages 3–5.**

A small child describes some of her fears and explains how she has become less fearful. Children will understand that fears are a normal and sometimes even necessary part of life.

Pfeffer, Susan Beth. *What Do You Do When Your Mouth Won't Open?* Delacorte Press, 1981. **Ages 10–13.**

A young girl with a deep fear of public speaking is helped to overcome her phobia in this lively first-person narrative. Although it seems odd that Reesa has never gotten help from parents or teachers and must seek it out herself, her encounters with the psychologist are convincing and the book's other relationships and situations ring true.

Fear of Physical Harm

Andersen, Karen Born. *What's the Matter, Sylvie, Can't you Ride?* The Dial Press, 1981. **Ages 4–7.**

Fear prevents Sylvie from learning to ride her new bicycle. Only when she gets reckless, so frustrated and angry that the possibility of physical harm is momentarily unimportant, does she conquer the bike. Though aimed at young readers, this story captures that familiar struggle between the drive to succeed and the fear of failure.

Fear of School

Delton, Judy. *A New Girl at School.* E. P. Dutton & Co., 1979. **Ages 4–7.**

Nervous about going to a new school, a little girl finds the adjustment difficult at first. But before too long she begins to make friends and feel at home—and soon there's a newer student than she.

Gross, Alan. *The I Don't Want to Go to School Book.* Children's Press, 1982. **Ages 5–9.**

This humorous look at a boy trying to evaluate the pros and cons of going to school will appeal to any reader who's ever had a bad day at school

Hogan, Paula Z. *Sometimes I Don't Like School.* Raintree Publishers, 1980. **Ages 6–9.**

Embarrassment about his poor performance in arithmetic clouds a young boy's feelings about school. He desperately tries to avoid the situation entirely; however, his understanding teacher recognizes his need for help. Once George admits his problem, he can and does take the necessary steps to solve it.

Lasker, Joe. *Nick Joins In.* Albert Whitman & Co., 1980. **Ages 5–8.**

A disabled child's initial fear of school dissolves with barely a ripple, thanks to understanding parents, sympathetic teachers, and his own outgoing attitude.

Quackenbush, Robert M. *First Grade Jitters.* J. B. Lippincott, 1982. **Ages 5–7.**

In this short, simple tale of apprehension about school, the young rabbit narrator feels defensive when his parents try to define his "jitters."

Tester, Sylvia Root. *We Laughed a Lot My First Day of School.* Children's Press, 1979. **Ages 3–6.**

A Mexican-American boy discovers that his fears about kindergarten are unfounded, and he enjoys a positive first-day experience.

Fear of Separation

Helmering, Doris Wild. *I Have Two Families.* Abingden Press, 1981. **Ages 6–8.**

This timely first-person narrative, told by Patty, shows that children can live a normal life after their parents' divorce. Patty and Michael experience all the fears and uncertainties that most children of divorce feel.

Schuchman, Joan. *Two Places to Sleep.* Carolrhoda Books, 1979. **Ages 5–7.**

David is uncertain and fearful about his parents' divorce. Despite patient, supportive, reassuring parents, a young boy needs time and abundant love to accept the break-up of his family.

Fear of Storms

Sussman, Susan. *Hippo Thunder.* Albert Whitman & Co, 1982. **Ages 3–6.**

A little boy learns a simple and relatively accurate trick for overcoming his fear of thunder.

Zolotow, Charlotte. *The Storm Book.* Harper & Row, 1952. **Ages 5–9.**

The scariness and eventual beauty of a storm and its aftermath are described to help the young reader cope with fear of storms.

Fear of the Unknown

Calhoun, Mary Huiskamp. *The Night the Monster Came.* William Morrow & Co, 1982. **Ages 8–10.**

Andy "cries wolf" several times before the monster he sees, a wounded bear, impels him to consider the safety of others as he overcomes his fear and traps the animal.

Hogan, Paul Z and Kirk. *The Hospital Scares Me.* Raintree Publishers, 1980. **Ages 3–8.**

This reassuring, simple, but informative account of a little boy's surgery and hospital stay could help prepare children for a hospital visit or be useful in describing the hospital experience to a child's siblings or classmates.

Lipp, Frederick J. *Some Lose Their Way.* Atheneum Publishers, 1980. **Ages 10–13.**

Two lonely young 8th graders find their way past the misconceptions they have about each other to form an enduring, nourishing friendship. Natural history becomes an integral part of the story.

Wartski, Maureen Crane. *The Lake is on Fire.* The Westminster Press, 1981. **Ages 10–13.**

A boy's numb despair over his own blindness and the death of his friend lifts when he embarks on a dangerous trek through a burning forest, forced to rely on the eyes of the dog he fears.

Appendix 1-D: Resource List

Books

Brenner, A. (1984). *Helping children cope with stress.* Lexington, MA: Lexington Books, $10.95.

For teachers and those who work with children under stress.

Canfield, J., & Wells, H. (1976). *100 ways to enhance self-concept in the classroom: A handbook for teachers and parents.* Paperbacks for Educators, 426 West Front Street, Washington, MO 63090, $21.95.

K–adult: Self-esteem building activities.

Doyle, P., & Behrens, D. (1986). *The child in crisis.* Paperbacks for Educators, 426 West Front St., Washington, MO 63090, $17.95.

For teachers/counselors to help children cope with personal crisis.

Dreyer, S. (1985). *The bookfinder: When kids need books.* American Guidance Service, Publishers Building, Circle Pines, MN 55014; $19.95 softcover; $54.95 hardcover.

Reference volume of children's books by author, title and topic or subject.

Faber, A., & Mazlish, E. (1980). *How to talk so kids will listen and listen so kids will talk.* Paperbacks for Educators, 426 West Front St., Washington, MO 63090, $6.95.

For parents, teachers, counselors and administrators.

Freericks, M., & Segal, J. (1979). *Creative puppetry in the classroom.* Rowayton, CT: New Plays Books.

Illustrations and instructions for puppet making.

Graver, C. M., & Morse, L. (1986). *Helping children of divorce: A group leader's guide.* Springfield, IL: Charles C. Thomas, $19.75.

For educators/counselors to help elementary students cope with divorce.

Gregson, B. (1982). *The incredible indoor games book.* Paperbacks for Educators, 426 West Front St., Washington, MO 63090, $11.95.

Grades K–8: Guidance, team-building, communication and cooperation.

Lesesne, T. S. (1986). *I'm special: A program for 4th graders.* The Drug Education Center, 1416 E. Morehead, Charlotte, NC 28204, $9.50.

Grades 3–5: Unit of activities to build self-esteem, communication and decision-making skills.

McCullough, C. J., & Mann, R. W. (1985). *Managing your anxiety.* Jeremy P. Tarcher, Inc., 9110 Sunset Blvd., Los Angeles, CA 90069, $15.95.

Stress management.

McKnew, D. H., Jr., Cytryn, L., & Yahraes, H. (1983). *Why isn't Johnnie crying? Coping with depression in children.* W. W. Norton, 500 Fifth Ave., New York, NY 10110, $15.50.

Depression in young children.

Myrick, R., & Bowman, R. (1981).

Becoming a friendly helper: A handbook for student facilitators. Educational Media Corp., Box 21311, Minneapolis, MN 55421, $4.95.

Children helping children: Teaching students to become friendly helpers. Educational Media Corp., Box 21311, Minneapolis, MN 55421, $9.95.

Grades 5–8: Peer counseling, manuals for trainers and students.

Renfro, N. (1979). *Puppetry and the art of story creation.* Austin, TX: Nancy Renfro Studios.

Comprehensive, illustrated guide to puppetry.

Robinson, J. (1985). *Culture shock: Information packet for developing stress/culture shock programs for students in overseas schools.* ERIC Document Reproduction Service No. ED 249 430.

Sarafino, E. (1985). *The fears of childhood: A guide to recognizing and reading fearful states in children.* Human Sciences Press, 72 Fifth Ave., New York, NY 10011-8004, $3.95.

For teachers and administrators.

Stanish, B. (1982). *Connecting rainbows.* Paperbacks for Educators, 426 West Front St., Washington, MO 63090, $8.95.

Grades 3–8: Self-esteem, values, cooperation and communication.

Stroebel, C. F. (1982). *QR: The quieting reflex.* New York: Berkley Books.

Relaxation training.

Thomas, M. (1987). *Free to be...a family.* Paperbacks for Educators, 426 West Front St., Washington, MO 63090, $19.95 hardcover.

For use with all ages in school or at home. Contains poems, songs and stories about belonging.

U.S. Department of State. (1986). *Managing children during a crisis.* Washington, DC: Author.

Walczak, Y., & Burns, S. (1984). *Divorce: The child's point of view.* Harper & Row, 28 Tavistock St., London, UK NC2E7PN, $8.00.

Children's reactions to divorce.

Weinstein, M., & Goodman, J. (1980). *Playfair: Everybody's guide to noncompetitive play.* Paperbacks for Educators, 426 West Front St., Washington, MO 63090, $9.95.

Grades 4–adult: Team-building and cooperation.

Multimedia

Antonucci, P., Schumacher, S., & Travers, L. (1986). *Biofeedback microlab.* HRM Software, Room MI-78910, 175 Tompkins Ave., Pleasantville, NY 10570, $350.00 for disk, interface box, sensors and guide.

Grades 6–adult: For students/teachers to provide firsthand feedback to the body's reaction to stress.

Bowman, R. P. (1987). *Test buster pep rally.* Educational Media Corp., P.O. Box 21311, Minneapolis, MN 55421, $79.95.

Grades K–6: Test-taking strategies and stress reduction.

Christesen, B., & Vanderslice, C. (1984). *Who am I? Looking at self-concept.* Sunburst Communications, Inc., 39 Washington Ave., Pleasantville, NY 10570-9971, $109.00.

2 filmstrips/2 cassettes: self-esteem enhancement.

Coping with family changes. Sunburst Communications, 101 Castleton St., Pleasantville, NY 10570-9971, $165.00

Grades 6–9: Filmstrips/cassette or videocassette.

Davis, D. E., (1988). *My friends and me.* American Guidance Service, Circle Pines, MN 55014-1796, ranges from $12.95 to $285.00 for entire guidance kit, components separate.

Guidance kit: 4, 5 and 6 year olds.

Dinkmeyer, D., Sr., & Dinkmeyer, D., Jr. (1982). *DUSO-Revised: Developing understanding of self and others.* American Guidance Service, Circle Pines, MN 55014-1796, $149.00 to $249.00.

Guidance kit: grades K–4.

Dupont, H., & Dupont, C. (1979). *Transition.* American Guidance Service, Circle Pines, MN 55014-1796, $242.50.

Guidance kit: grades 6–9.

Dupont, H., Gardner, O. S., & Brody, D. S. (1974). *TAD: Toward affective development.* American Guidance Service, Circle Pines, MN 55014-1796, $249.00.

Guidance kit: grades 3–6.

Einstein, E. I., & Albert, L. (1986). *Strengthening step-families.* American Guidance Service, Circle Pines, MN 55014-1796, $89.50.

Parent education program with audiotapes and other components: 5-session program.

Hendricks, G. *The centered student: Stress & relaxation.* Learning Tree Filmstrips, P.O. Box 4116, Englewood, CO 80155, $99.00.

Grades 3–6: 8 audiocassettes and guide; self-confidence, creativity, handling stress.

Herzfeld, G., & Powell, R. (1986). *Coping for kids: A complete stress-control program for students ages 8–18.* Center for Applied Research in Education, P.O. Box 430, West Nyack, NY 10995, $39.95.

Managing stress.

Learning to say no. (1985). Sunburst Communications, 101 Castleton St., Pleasantville, NY 10570-9971, $119.00 filmstrip/cassette; $139.00 videocassette.

Grades 4–6: refusal and assertiveness skills.

Palmer, H. (1973). *Sea gulls* [Recording]. Freeport, NY: Educational Activities.

Background music for relaxation.

Popkin, M. H. (1983). *Active parenting.* American Guidance Service, Circle Pines, MN 55014-1796, $295.00.

Parenting education program with videocassette and other components, 6-session program.

Stroebel, E., Stroebel, C. F., & Holland, M. (1980). *Kiddie QR: A choice for children.* QR Institute, 119 Forest Drive, Wethersfield, CT 06109.

Relaxation training tapes and manuals.

Thomas, M. (1979). *Free to be...you and me* [Recording]. New York: McGraw-Hill.

Songs to learn about self and others.

Part 2

Facilitator's Guide

Introduction

In order to ensure a successful workshop, it is important to be keenly aware of your audience, their knowledge and sensitivity to the topic, and the way you establish a working relationship with them. One of the best ways to make certain that you are successful is to be as prepared as possible for your workshop. This includes understanding the topic and having a stimulating approach to delivering the material.

Knowing Your Audience

The teachers in your workshop will have had a range of experiences in dealing with children's fear and stress. It is important, therefore, not to insult your audience by overstating or undershooting their level of knowledge or skill. This is impossible to avoid 100% of the time, but there are ways of checking these extremes before beginning or, at the latest, at the beginning of your workshop. First of all, you can use the fear and stress survey instrument in Appendix 2-A (page 165) of this guide to determine the level of knowledge regarding the subject and use the results in preparing the agenda of activities. If this is not possible, the instrument or a modified version could be administered as one of the first activities of the workshop. In addition, an agenda-setting time can be spent at the beginning of the workshop which would take into consideration the needs and desires of the participants. This does not mean that you do not come prepared, but it allows for individual differences. You need to operate on the premise of "rigid flexibility"—rigid to the extent that you have specific goals to achieve, and flexible in the way you achieve them.

Eight-Session Design

The eight-session design is intended to accommodate several training configurations. For example, the eight one-and-one-half hour sessions can be delivered in a two-day format or by session after school over an extended period of time. The suggested design can be modified to meet local needs but reducing the time devoted to the total training or a given component could reduce the effectiveness of the preparation. The outline which follows will be presented as a two-day workshop with the one-and-one-half hour blocks defined for easy focus should an alternative workshop format be chosen.

Session 1: Introduction

The purpose of this session is to provide an opportunity for the participants to briefly share something about themselves and establish an atmosphere of relaxed sharing.

The opening session should begin with an introductory activity. You may wish to devise some activity that would involve the entire group to engender some cohesiveness and focus their attention on the topic. If you are working in a school where the staff is small and are well acquainted a simple "go around" activity where you ask each person to share a feeling about being in the workshop and to state why they are interested in the topic is a good beginning. If you are working with a large group or where there are many strangers a more in-depth "get acquainted" activity may be needed, such as Human Bingo.

Human Bingo is a fun activity that allows people to discover and share things about themselves and each other by identifying characteristics of others in the group. Each participant is given a Human Bingo card with characteristics identified in each square. Give them 15 minutes to go around the room, identify one person for each characteristic and ask that person to initial the square that matches their characteristic. The first person who completes the card is recognized and then others are recognized by the number of squares completed. The participants are encouraged to get as many different signatures as possible. Here is a sample Human Bingo card. You will want to include items of local interest in the blank squares.

Human Bingo

From Northeastern State	Likes Chocolate	Plays Bridge	
Likes to Snow Ski	Exercises Daily		
Does Yoga			

If the group is acquainted, an activity called Know Your Place will both physically energize the group and introduce them to the topic. Know your Place is an activity which allows the participants to explore their environment which is in itself often the source of fear and stress. In fact, it is an excellent exercise for use with children. Becoming acquainted with the nuances of one's surroundings can alleviate much potential fear and stress by exposing the fear object for what it is. This activity simply asks the participants to move around the room in silence exploring its contents and composition. Ask them to look under, around, behind, and in things. Ask them to note unusual characteristics about the room and its contents. After 5 minutes of silent exploration ask them to take a seat and share with the larger group what they discovered. After the discussion ask them, while seated, to take one more sweeping look around the room.

There are many other ways of asking the group to get acquainted with each other and the topic. Be creative and use whatever you think will be effective, but by all means include some activity that will set the stage for comfort and sharing.

After the getting acquainted activity, you are ready to begin your study of children's fear and stress. And, one of the first items you want to address is the source of one's own fear and stress. It is at this point that the earlier "get acquainted" activity becomes significant, for they are now going to be asked to take a greater risk by sharing some of their own experiences with fear and stress. This also helps to personalize the experience while at the same time sharpening awareness of the problems related to fear and stress. This can be accomplished in several ways. However, a way that has proven effective is to encourage teachers to focus on real situations.

With a focus on personalizing the activity, it is necessary for you to be aware of and use the uniqueness of the situation. For example, if you are in an exceptionally contained situation, where limits are placed on movement within the community, this may pose different fears and stress than in a more open setting. The activity which follows is intended as an "icebreaker" and serves as an indirect introduction to the topic. The idea is to get the participants hooked on the subject of fear and stress by tapping their own experience and imagination.

Activity

Title: Fear and Stress Assessment

Purpose: To help participants identify unresolved fears and stress.

Outcomes:
1. Recognize how their own fears may be relevant to how they relate to children's fears.
2. Recognize coping strategies used to address fear and stress.

Materials: Fear and Stress Assessment Form (FASAF)

Procedures:
1. Ask participants to study FASAF (see page 127).
2. Have participants identify a real student fear and stress and complete the form up to the dotted vertical line.
3. Break group into dyads and ask them to briefly discuss the student fear and stress they identified on the FASAF.

4. Ask the teachers to reflect upon their own early experiences as they relate to the student fear or stress identified on the form and complete the final three sections of the FASAF.
5. Ask the teachers to again discuss their findings in dyads.
6. Allow time for sharing with the entire group. As this can be a sensitive situation, sharing should be strictly on a voluntary basis.

Overview

After completing the FASAF activity you will want to give a brief overview of the training and specifically focus on Session 1. At the beginning of each session it is important to provide an overview. This in itself is an excellent means of allaying some fear or stress with the participants, as was pointed out earlier with the Know Your Place activity. It is also important to conduct a warm-up activity. You will find a suggested warm-up activity at the beginning of each session. Again, these are only suggestions, but it is important that some type of warm-up activity be included.

A suggested overview for Session 1 follows:

"The purpose of today's session is to begin to explore the typical fears and stress of children. You will be asked to voluntarily share some of your own experiences with the topic and how you deal with fear and stress and help children deal with theirs. In addition, we will take some time to discuss a tested model for identifying and treating fear and stress in children. Finally, we will spend some time looking at the sources and signs of stress and fear. In the sessions that follow today we will be exploring some specific approaches that can be used in the classroom to help children take control of their fears and stress. The classroom suggestions are designed to be infused into the academic curriculum and, therefore, will not add to your already busy schedule. In fact, if implemented, the benefits of helping children deal with their fears and stress can only enhance their focus upon the academic curriculum."

You may wish to elaborate on this suggested overview to fit your situation.

Agenda Setting

Since each school setting is unique and the manifested fears and stress are likewise unique, it is important to take time early on during the first session to allow for some agenda setting on the part of the teachers. This agenda setting should take place after you have provided the overview. If not, you may not get any response or you may end up with an agenda that is totally foreign to your purpose. In other words, you need to establish the basic purpose for the training and then, within those parameters, allow for the uniqueness of the setting or individual concerns. When accepting agenda items make certain that they are ones that are acceptable to the group and not just one person's issues. If people bring up personal concerns that are not appropriate to the group you may offer to talk with them privately and be prepared to make referrals if necessary. This is a remote possibility, but when dealing with this topic there is always the chance that individual concerns will emerge.

Model

Once the agenda has been set you will want to give an overview of the model for identifying and treating fear and stress (see Section 1 of Part 1: Discussion and Activities). The strategies and developmental interventions will be addressed during a later session. At this point you want them to develop a grasp of the development of fears and stress and help them to understand the fear and stress cycle. You may wish to make a transparency of Figure 1-1 on page 6 to assist you in your brief overview of the model.

After presenting the model you will need to discuss the sources and signs of stress. If the Fears and Stress Survey (FSS) on page 165 was completed in advance you will want to ask the group to discuss in small groups of five or six members each the responses they made on the survey. If you are introducing the FSS during this session, allow time for the teachers to complete it and then discuss in small groups.

You are referred to "Sources of Fear in Children" from page 6. You will want to share these data with the group and make comparisons with their responses. Do not share the information from the guide until the group has completed the FSS and discussed their responses in their small groups.

A brief overview of what will take place during the next session is appropriate here before adjourning.

Session 1
Outline

I.	Opening activity Explore environment, train station, or human bingo	20 minutes
II.	Recollection of early childhood fears (see FSAF, page 127) Overview Agenda setting	15 minutes
III.	Discuss model (include assessment instrument if not completed prior to workshop) Sources and signs of fear and stress (feedback on FSS if used)	25 minutes See Table 1-1 (Normative Data on Children's Fears), page 8

Fear and Stress Assessment Form (FSAF)

Identify a Situation or incident that is a source of fear or stress in your setting	Affect How you felt?	Cognition What you told yourself?	Behavior How did you respond to the client?	Self-Perception Success or failure	Insights Related personal or past experiences	Current Impact Still a stressor?	Coping Who or what helped?
Example: 1. Student comes in upset about a friend's death	Helpless, overwhelmed by student's emotion	I need to get this student to stop crying	Non-supportive, I did not validate student's feelings	Failure	Unresolved grief over my own mother's death	Yes	It helped to talk with a colleague and do this assessment

Session 2: Primary Prevention

The purpose of this session is to address the three levels of primary prevention as presented in Figure 2-1 (page 130). An overview of the levels will be discussed followed by an in-depth study of the first level of prevention and related intervention strategies.

Warm-up Activity

Ask the teachers to sit comfortably, close their eyes if they choose, and imagine a small wooden or metal box or safe. The box is made of sturdy material with a hinged lid that can be secured by a padlock. Ask them to gather all of the bits and pieces of unfinished business and place them one by one in the box, e.g., a leaky faucet at home, questions like, "Did I turn off the iron?", "Will I have electricity when I get home tonight?", "Will I get my papers graded tonight?" Take all of these loose ends and unrelated issues to today's session and place them securely in the box. Then ask them to secure the padlock to lock the box holding these items for safekeeping until they choose to remove them. Have them place the key in a safe place for retrieval later. Now that all these issues are safely stored, tell them they can focus entirely on today's topic without interference. After they have completed this fantasy ask them to open their eyes and continue to maintain their comfortable position.

This activity will help them to focus on the topic at hand by temporarily ridding them of all the potential external interferences. It also allows them to relax and focus on a collective activity. This activity can be modified for use with students to help them with concentration (Tubesing & Tubesing, 1986).

Levels of Prevention

Three levels of prevention are presented in the fear and stress model represented in Figure 2-1 (see page 130). Level 1 focuses on the normative fears and stress of childhood, such as, fear of the dark, first day of school, or moving to a new city state or country. The emphasis in level one is not on the fears but on preventive approaches to help children develop the concepts of control, security, and self-worth.

The activities from Sections 2 and 3 in Part 1 should be introduced during this session. Select one of the fear specific and one of the fear prevention activities and demonstrate with the group. Ask the teachers to again tap their imaginations and fantasize a classroom situation as they participate in the activities.

In the discussion which follows the fear specific activity, point out the difference between episodic fears or situational stress and generalized fears or chronic stress. Episodic fears such as moving to a new city or changing schools can be addressed

FEAR OBJECT

PREVENTION	PREVENTION	PREVENTION
DEVELOPMENTAL	HIGH RISK	TREATMENT
CONTROL	SECURITY	SELF-WORTH

Figure 2-1
Primary Prevention of Children's Fears

specifically while generalized fears, such as fear of strangers, are more difficult to observe. Each, however, can be anticipated and preventive approaches can be used to alleviate the potential chronic long term problems that can be manifested. The long term effects of fear and stress can in fact be debilitating emotionally and physically. Withdrawal from certain activities and development of physical ailments can result if appropriate skills and attitudes are not established early in life.

Level 1 approaches to the prevention of the debilitating effects of fear and stress are, therefore, significant to the way children will learn to deal with events throughout their lives. The focus here is on problem solving and decision making, two critical skills for dealing with both episodic and generalized fear and stress. Children who develop effective problem solving and decision making skills will recognize that they have control over their lives and therefore will experience a greater sense of security and self-worth both in school and elsewhere. According to Norman Sprinthall, the whole point of the concept of primary prevention is, "...to create classroom educative experiences that affect student's intellectual and personal development simultaneously" (Gerler, 1986).

References

Gerler, E. R., & Anderson, R. F. (1986). The effects of classroom guidance on children's success in school. *Journal of Counseling and Development, 65,* 78–81.

Tubesing, N. L., & Tubesing, D. A. (1986). *Structural exercises in stress management.* Duluth, MN: Whole Person Press.

Session 2
Outline

I.	Activity	10 minutes
II.	Levels of Prevention Primary Prevention High Risk Non-coping	20 minutes See Figure 2-1, page 130 (Primary Prevention of Children's Fears)
III.	Primary Prevention Activities Episodic fears and stress, e.g., moving to new city; Generalizable fears and stress, e.g., fear of the dark	45 minutes See Figure 1-1, page 6 (Fear Cycle)
IV.	Decision-Making and Problem-Solving Skills	15 minutes

Session 3: School and Classroom Activities

The purpose of this session is to help teachers and other school personnel develop ideas for activities that they can do with children to help them in developing the knowledge and skills necessary for coping with fear and stress. A further purpose is to help school personnel understand the way environment can contribute to fear and stress and develop strategies to help children cope.

Overview

The session should be opened with an activity from Part 1: Discussion and Activities. Pick an activity that you think participants will enjoy that can relate to a number of different curriculum areas. The "Peruvian Worry Dolls" for instance can relate to art, geography, social studies, foreign language, etc. The activity helps children learn to cope with fear and stress by learning to verbalize their worries. A number of research studies support the positive effects of cathartic release when dealing with stress or fear by just "getting it off your chest." Not all people have someone close at hand to talk to in such cases. Talking to a worry doll can help a person sort it out in a similar way to journal or diary writing. A variation is to record your talk to your worry doll and play back your talk once or twice a week.

Discuss how the activity can be used in the classroom not only to develop coping for fear or stress but also as a part of class contact. Art: The dolls can be made of ceramics, cloth, paper, paper mache, almost anything. Concepts in art are many: different colors, principles of sculpting, etc. Social Studies: The activities can be used as a vehicle for discussing South America, the customs and nature of the people of Peru, etc. Language: parts of the body, days of the week, articles of clothing, etc. For time here make only one doll.

After the activity, break the group into small groups by grade level or subject matter. Have them find three other activities in Part 1: Discussion and Activities that they could integrate into the curriculum. Have each group report to the whole group on the activities they discussed and share how they could use the activity as a part of the subject matter they are teaching.

Take a minute to talk about how many of the activities can be used in a curriculum way that does not take away time from the subject to be taught. Also discuss the idea that you may want to do some activities just because they may help children develop ways of coping with fear and stress. A child who cannot concentrate on the learning task at hand because of the level of stress or the fear that they can't deal with is not actively engaged in learning. Helping them deal with their problems can increase the time on task for learning. Remember time on task is not the time the teacher spends teaching. Time on task is the time the child spends learning. Ten to twenty minutes a day spent building wellness in children can have tremendous benefits in cognitive learning. Research indicates that children who jog before class each day, learn relaxation techniques, learn to communicate and make friends, develop confidence in self, learn effective personal decision making, etc., do better on cognitive tasks in the classroom.

Break into small groups and ask participants to brainstorm those things about the school or community that is stressful for children. Discuss these in the whole group. After tests, studies will likely be mentioned. The very structure of the school can be stressful. Most schools are competitive in nature stressing individual goals and the concept of winners and losers.

To underline this idea have everyone line up in a straight line. After they are all lined up say, "OK, we're going to have a spelling bee." Ask the first person in line to spell cat, the next person dog, the next jump, etc. Ask the fourth or fifth person to spell lactobacillus. Before they get embarrassed call off the spelling bee. The spelling bee is the perfect example of an individual competitive environment. Some children thrive on this type of environment, others give up to avoid the stress and fear of failure, embarrassment, etc. Others turn the stress inward. Too much competition, a lot of losers and few winners. While there may always be a place for competition, the research is very strong that cooperative learning decreases stress and increases learning outcomes. Show how the spelling bee could become "cooperative competitive"—two or more groups competing with each other but on a cooperative team, i.e., divide class into three groups, each person must spell a word, but that person may consult with two members of their group before spelling the word. You can be a consultant once every 2-3-4 times. A number of reactions are possible. Now show how spelling can be a completely cooperative venture. "Last week we had ten spelling words, we have ten people in the class. Ten words were spelled correctly for the whole class. This week we will work for 75 words correct. I have divided the class into study groups. Your task is to help everyone learn the words for Friday." (If intrinsic motivation is not enough). If we get 75 we will...(appropriate extrinsic motivator). If not, we will try again next week.

Human Spring: to underline the concept ask people if they have ever done leg wrestling or arm wrestling. Two people competing: at the end, a winner who feels good about his or her participation and a loser. Have class pair up for human spring: stand about 2–3 feet apart, pull up hands, palms out toward partner; each person leans into his or her partner so that both are off balance but sustained by each other like a pyramid or triangle; push each other back to a standing position; increase the distance between each other and try again. The goal is to see how far apart two people can get and still help each other return to a standing position without anyone losing their balance. No one loses; each pair is working to accomplish a goal together.

Take a minute to brainstorm how the classroom and or school could do more cooperative learning and play activities to decrease stress.

What other environmental stressors did you discuss earlier? What else can the group come up with to deal with these? (You may wish to carry this discussion over to Session 8.)

Materials

Materials needed for group activity include Peruvian Worry Dolls (enough materials to make one doll per participant; for time restraints you may wish to make dolls out of paper in which case you will need paper, scissors, crayons, gluesticks; you may want to use Popsicle type sticks to glue to dolls as stand). Socks can also be used quickly with stuffing material, crayons for face and hair, etc. and something to close the open end (string, ribbon, rubber bands, tread, etc.).

Bibliography

Johnson, D., & Johnson, R. (1986). *Circles of learning*. Englewood Cliffs, NJ: Prentice Hall.

Johnson, D., & Johnson, R. (1987). *Learning together and alone*. Englewood Cliffs, NJ: Prentice Hall.

Weinstein, M., & Goodman, J. (1981). *Play fare*. CA: Impact Press.

New Games Institute. (1979). *New games*.

Session 3
Outline

I.	Activity from Part 1: Discussion and Activities (Peruvian Worry Dolls, etc.)	30 minutes
II.	Discussion on how activities can be used for fear and stress as well as in subject areas. Pick out several other activities from Part 1 and discuss how they can be used.	10 minutes
III.	Small group brainstorming on Environmental Stressors	10 minutes
IV.	Spelling Bee	10 minutes
V.	Discussion—Competition vs. Cooperation	15 minutes
VI.	Human Spring	5 minutes
VII.	Discussion Other environmental stressors and how might you deal with them?	10 minutes

Session 4: Helping High Risk Children

The purpose of this session is to help teachers and other school personnel recognize potential high risk children and to develop the knowledge and skills necessary for helping these children.

Overview

High risk children are those who are more susceptible to fear and stress and more likely to suffer possible ill effects of fear or stress. Children who move to a new area for the first time, children whose language is not the language of instruction, children whose parents are separated or divorced, children who have experienced traumatic events or disasters, children whose values or culture place a great deal of emphasis on specific behaviors or goals such as academic success as measured by grades or test scores, children with learning difficulties, etc.

Start off the session with an activity that highlights one of these groups, e.g., children for which the language of instruction is not their native language. An activity that can be used is to ask half the group to leave the room for a minute and wait just outside. Give the remaining participants instructions to tell the person they are paired with when the others return to do a simple task. (Write your name on the board, put that piece of paper in the trash can, give me your book, spell the word cat, etc.) These tasks must be spoken in a foreign language. If the individual knows a language that their partner does not know they may use that language, otherwise be creative and make up a word "Dr. Seuss style" for each word in the instructions. For example, "put that piece of paper in the trash can" could be written "Urn dar cue vo yerd we na dina tur." You may wish to have several of these already made up on a slip of paper. Tell the people who will assign the task to be forceful and act as if the person should know what you are saying. If they don't respond, say it louder and be even more demanding. Give people a minute to memorize the new language then ask the others to rejoin the group. Have the participants pair off: one to assign the task paired with one who has been out of the room. Explain to the "outsiders" that they will be asked to perform a simple classroom task that any third grader can do and they will repeat the task until it is done or until time is called.

Give the participant a few minutes: five or six repeats of the task. Some will probably give hints through body language. Stop the activity and let people settle back in their seats to discuss the activity. How did you feel knowing it was a simple task but not knowing what was said? How did you look for hints on what to do? Have you ever been anywhere where you did not know the language and you were trying to figure out what to do? How was your stress level in such a situation? Why is it a stressful situation?

Define "At Risk Children" with the group and brainstorm groups of children at your school that may fall into this category.

Break into groups and discuss ways to help the at risk child, e.g., a student who is facing a new place, new school, and new people. Just because someone has done it before doesn't mean it's not stressful. Uprooting someone's routine is often hard on adults, but it can be just as hard on children. Little things we don't think about can be stressful: How do I get my lunch? where do I put my books? and so on. You can assign a friendly helper to show a new student the routine. You can ask that new students not be brought to the room and dropped off in the middle of the day. Tell parents to please bring their child back first thing in the morning because you would like time to make arrangements for his or her first day. This gives the teacher time to prepare and to plan to make the new student feel really welcome.

Give groups time to discuss strategies they might use. Use Appendix 1-A, page 103, as a vehicle.

Bring the groups back together and ask them to share their discussions with the whole group.

Introduce the concept of the single child at risk. This is a child that doesn't fit any categories the school defines as "at risk" but is, nonetheless, a child under a lot of stress. What are the signs of stress for a child? How can you tell that a child is under stress? You may wish to brainstorm this question before you pass out the list of signs of stress in children.

Materials

Strips of paper with directions for simple classroom tasks written in English and in a foreign or made up language. Blackboard or chart, holder with chart paper for brainstorming ideas and recording.

Bibliography

Adams, J. D. (1980). *Understanding and managing stress: A facilitators guide.* San Diego: University Associates.

Miller, S. M. (1982). *Child stress: Understanding and answering stress signals of infants, children, and teenagers.* Garden City, NY: Doubleday.

Schultz, E., & Hurchurt, C. (1983). *Childhood Stress and the School Experience.* New York: Human Science Press.

Stroebel, E., & Stroebel, C. (1980). *Kiddie QR: A choice for children.* Wethersfield, CT: QR Institute.

Session 4
Outline

I.	Activity (Simple classroom task in foreign languages)	20 minutes
II.	Discuss Activity	10 minutes
III.	Define "At Risk Children" and present example; Brainstorm groups of at-risk children	10 minutes
IV.	Present example of how you might help one at-risk group (new student); Break into groups and brainstorm strategies for other at-risk groups	20 minutes
V.	Small Group Sharing Strategies	10 minutes
VI.	Discuss concept of the single child at risk and the signs of stress	20 minutes

Session 5: Helping Children During a Crisis

The purpose of this session is to help teachers develop an understanding of how to help children cope with their fears and stress during a crisis. A crisis might include a collective crisis, such as the assassination of a political leader or natural disaster such as an earthquake, or an individual crisis like the loss of a parent.

Overview

Open the session with an activity. One suggestion is to pass out a piece of clay to everyone in the group and ask them to hold the clay. Tell them they may play with it as they see fit while you talk (they are not allowed to throw it, however). Ask people to close their eyes and remember back with you to the year 1963. Picture a day in your life: November 22, 1963. What were you doing on that day? What images do you have of that day? Continue imaging with participants the events of the assassination of President Kennedy and the days following. If the group is younger you might use April 29-30, 1975: picture the U.S. embassy in Saigon or some other event that most would share. These are collectively shared events. Each person reacts a bit differently but most have strong emotional memories. Notice what people do with the clay as you go through the recollection process. Ask participants if they were aware of what they did with the clay (some will probably just hold it, some will just knead it, some may make shapes or forms).

Discussion: One teacher used clay at story time to help children deal with the stress of a crisis around them. Teachers would pass out clay, give children a chance to talk about what was going on around them, and then read a story. As the days went by children would knead less and begin making things with the clay. Clay and play can be a great tension release for children.

During and after a crisis or traumatic event it is important to keep to a routine but not ignore the events or the feelings people have about the events surrounding them. It is important that you let children have the opportunity to discuss or express their feelings about the crisis. It is also important not to dwell on events: answer factual questions with accurate factual responses. A crisis often reminds children what little control they have over their lives and leaves them feeling vulnerable. Emphasize the control they do have. "It seems you handled that well. I see you are sorting this mess out," and so on.

Hand out Appendix 2-B (page 167) to the group. Break into small groups. Have each grade level or appropriate group (primary, intermediate, etc.) meet together and discuss the handouts. How would they give emotional first aid to children this age? Verbal catharsis can be difficult for preschool or kindergarten children. Expressing their feelings through art or play might be better.

Give the small groups an additional task of determining what to do after the crisis to help children. Although the emotions of a crisis will be dissipating, the "after crisis" emotions can still be strong. Look through Part 1: Discussion and Activities and discuss activities that would be helpful to your age group in dealing with the aftermath of a traumatic event.

In the groups have teachers share how they help children deal with personal crisis such as the loss of a parent. Read *The Fall of Freddie, The Leaf* or another book that talks about death and discusses how books can be used with children to help them cope.

End the session with a relaxation activity. You can use the scripts from Part 1 on pages 82 and 87 or develop your own. You can use guided imagery or physical relaxation or a combination. This could be helpful in a crisis and/or as a preventive technique that can help people on a day-to-day basis.

Materials

Script for opening exercise and clay; script for relaxation activity; book or chart for recording if desired; handouts from Appendix 2-B.

Bibliography

Crabbs, M. A. (1981). School mental health services following an environmental disaster. *Journal of School Health, 51,* 165–167.

Farberow, N., & Gordon, N. S. (1981). *Manual for child health worker in major disaster.* Washington, DC: U.S. Department of Health and Human Services, National Institute of Mental Health, U.S. Government Printing Office. (DHHS Publication No. ADM 81-1070)

Rotter, J. C., & Robinson, E. H. (1987). Coping with fear and stress: Classroom intervention. *International Quarterly, 5*(4), 39–45.

Schwarcz, J. H. (1982). Guiding children's creative expression in the stress of war. *Stress and Anxiety, 8,* 351–354.

Session 5
Outline

I.	Activity: Remember When	10 minutes
II.	Mini Lecture-Discussion Tips on Helping Children in a Crisis	15 minutes
III.	Small Group Activity Handouts: Emotional First Aid Developmental Differences	20 minutes
IV.	Small Group Activity After the First Aid	10 minutes
V.	Activity: Read book on loss; give examples of reflection discussion questions that might be used	10 minutes
VI.	Discussion: How do teachers help children in personal crisis?	10 minutes
VII.	Relaxation and/or guided imagery activity	10 minutes

Session 6: Helping Children Who Are Not Coping Well

The purpose of this session is to help teachers and other school personnel develop an understanding of how to help children who are not coping well in their life because of the effects of fear and stress; to help teachers identify potential resources for helping children; and to provide strategies for those teachers who wish to help children work through their difficulties.

Overview

Begin the session by reviewing the prevention model discussed earlier in Session 1. The last stage of prevention is helping those children who are experiencing the effects of fear or stress in negative, self-defeating ways. The longer debilitating fears or stress go untreated, the harder they are to treat and the more likely they are to become worse and more disruptive in the child's life. Helping a child when fear first becomes disruptive can prevent worse problems and a deepening of the current problem.

Discuss the information presented in Section 1 of Part 1: Discussion and Activities. You may wish to ask participants to read this before the session. In the discussion, highlight the stages of helping a child with a fear-related problem. Point out the need for the child to be able to talk honestly and openly to someone they trust; someone that will not make fun of them or belittle their fears. Good general communication skills are needed here.

Also point out the importance of assessment. Is this a child with a fear *or* a fearful child? Although both need help, and many of the same activities or techniques may help both, the goal is slightly different as noted in the article. The teacher may help the fearful child deal with one fear to find it quickly replaced with another. Here the emphasis should be on helping the child develop a sense of worth, control, and security. On the other hand, a child may generally cope well but develop a fear of a specific object. Here help should be directed at coping with that specific fear.

Next, as a group, brainstorm the mental health resources of your community. Where can children get help with stress, fears and phobias? How can children in need be referred to these resources? What are the costs of these resources? Here the facilitator will want to do some homework on these questions before the group meets. Are there local counselors, psychologists, psychiatric social workers or nurses, or psychiatrists who are available to serve children with fear- and stress-related problems? Is there anyone else on the school staff trained and willing to help?

Next the facilitator may wish to conduct an activity for teachers to help them come to terms with the role they can play in helping children struggling with fears and stress. In some schools and communities there will be no help available. The teacher is truly the only mental health resource. In other cases the teacher will have additional resources. It is important for teachers to decide how much help they feel they can provide; what kinds of problems they feel trained to help with. You may wish to put these and other questions on a sheet of paper for each participant. Have participants fill them out individually then get together and have a discussion. Everyone can share the highlights of their group's discussion with the larger group. You may find a couple of teachers on each level who have had some counseling experience and who are willing to work with children or team up with teachers to help them work with children.

Present a mini lecture on the topic. If you are going to help, what do you do? Many of the fear prevention activities for high risk children in the classroom may be adapted to be appropriate for individual work. You may wish to suggest how several of these activities could be done. One of the most common techniques for helping children deal with extreme fear is systematic desensitization. A discussion of this is contained in Part 1 on page 97. Present this concept and demonstrate the procedure.

Discuss with the group when this might be a good approach with a child. Have the group pair off and role play or use a real fear if volunteered by one of the pairs. Practice establishing a hierarchy and the technique of systematic desensitization.

Materials

Information from Section 1 in Part 1: Discussion and Activities. Clarification sheet on questions teachers should ask.

Bibliography

Morris, R. J., & Kratochwill, T. R. (1983). *Treating children's fears and phobias.* New York: Pergamon Press.
Wolman, B. B. (1978). *Children's fears.* New York: Grosset and Dunlop.

Session 6
Outline

I. Mini Lecture and Discussion: 10 minutes
Review of primary prevention, counseling
model, stages of helping, fearful child or child
with a fear

II. Brainstorm and Discussion: Mental Health   5 minutes
Resources in School and Community

III. Teachers Role and Feelings of Competence   20 minutes
Clarification Activity

IV. Mini Lecture on Techniques of Helping   15 minutes
Individual Child With Fear and Stress

V. Presentation and Demonstration of   15 minutes
Systematic Desensitization (SD)

VI. Practice SD   25 minutes

Session 7: Stress/Fear and the Family

The purpose of this session is to emphasize that fear and stress are family issues. Although fear and stress may be triggered by isolated incidences, their effect on children often results from the amount of advance preparation that parents have made and their ability to effectively follow up on stressful situations.

Overview

This session is optional and may be incorporated in one of the other sessions. It is important, however, that parent involvement and family related issues be addressed at some time during the training. You may want to start a discussion with the teachers, then ask them to identify specific incidences they have encountered with crises or with which they are familiar. Ask them to share, in small groups, how an incident was handled and the effect it had on the children and the families involved.

It is often difficult to determine, during times of crisis, how much to share with children. This will vary depending on the age and developmental level of the child. However, it is important to keep the lines of communication open. Ignoring or minimizing an incident can cause more harm than a forthright discussion of the issues. Children who have established a sense of control, safety, and self-esteem will be able to deal with the situation knowing that they have a support system within the family and the community. When information is withheld or questions ignored, that support system becomes eroded.

The debilitating effects of stress and fear can be reduced, if not prevented, by taking care of oneself and maintaining the family as a unit. Through proper nutritional habits, regular exercise and some form of relaxation families can learn that taking care of themselves can serve as a very useful tool during a time of crisis (see Self-Management Techniques, page 154). Having a plan and maintaining open lines of communication can foster these necessary qualities of control, safety, and self-esteem essential for coping during times of stress.

In order to personalize the issues related to families and stress and fear, ask the teachers to take a moment to reflect upon their own family of origin. Ask them to recall the themes and values expressed within their families and to write down a family motto that was prevalent when they were growing up. Examples might include: "The family that plays together stays together." "Honesty is the best policy." When they have identified their family motto ask them to share it with the group. Next, begin a discussion of whether these mottos hold true for them and their families today. These mottos represent some very basic values that can have an impact on the way they conduct themselves in times of crisis.

Discuss the attachments located at the end of this session regarding family life cycle, family stresses, and family meetings. Finally, ask them to complete the Family Stressor Intervention Plan on page 151.

Bibliography

Arent, R. P. (1984). *Stress and your child.* Englewood Cliffs, NJ: Prentice Hall.

Curran, D. (1985). *Stress and the healthy family.* Minneapolis: Winston Press.

Elkind, D. (1981). *The hurried child: Growing up too fast too soon.* Reading, MA: Addison-Wesley.

Faber, A., & Mazlish, E. (1980). *How to talk so kids will listen and listen so kids will talk.* New York: Rawson, Wade Publishers.

Miller, S. M. (1982). *Childstress! Understanding and answering stress signals of infants, children and teenagers.* Garden City, NY: Doubleday.

United States Department of State. (1986). *Managing children during a crisis.* Washington, DC: Author.

Session 7
Outline

I.	Overview of Family Stress	15 minutes
II.	Small Group Discussion of Incidents	20 minutes
III.	Discuss Healthy Prevention Activities Proper Nutrition, Exercise, Relaxation (see Self-Management Techniques, page 154)	10 minutes
IV.	Family Motto Activity	10 minutes
V.	Discuss Family Life Cycle, Family Stresses and Family Meetings	15 minutes
VI.	Family Stressor Intervention Plan, page 151	20 minutes

Family Stressor Intervention Plan

Family stressors:

Target stressor:

Identify desired outcome:

Determine strategy:

Apply strategy:

Determine level of success:

What will be your next step?

Who will be involved?

Family Stressor Intervention Plan (Continued)

What will each person's (including yourself) role be?

What outside support systems are needed?

My personal time line—I will do the following:

Today

Tomorrow

Next Week

Ways to Mediate Family Stress

1. Establish family traditions.

2. Discuss family values.

3. Take on something bigger than yourself.

4. Respect differences within the family.

5. Emphasize wellness instead of illness.

6. Exercise together.

7. Allow for private time.

8. Become active in a community organization that includes children and adults.

9. Take on a family project.

10. Learn success imagery.

11. Turn problems into challenges.

12. Hold family meetings.

13. Develop and utilize effective communication skills.

14. Show that you care about and respect the other family members.

15. Go to entertainment together.

16. Provide a job within the family for *every* member.

17. Listen.

18. Emphasize cooperative dietary planning—adults setting good examples.

19. Eat one meal a day as a family to discuss day's events.

20. Laugh together.

Source: Rotter, M. F., & Rotter, J. C. (1985). *Stress is a family affair.* Presentation at AACD Convention, Los Angeles.

Self-Management Techniques

Good Nutritional Habits

1. Balanced diet

    a. Sufficient vitamins, minerals, protein, complex carbohydrates and fiber

    b. Minimized consumption of sugar, salt, saturated fats, refined white flour and chemical additives

2. Regular meals

3. Maintenance of recommended weight

4. Moderate use of alcohol and caffeine

5. No smoking

Good Exercise Habits

1. Regular aerobic exercise to improve cardiovascular fitness

2. Regular recreational exercise for tension reduction and diversion

Self-Awareness

1. Understanding of personal needs, preferences and idiosyncrasies

2. Assertive behavior and role negotiation

Letting Go Techniques

1. Regular relaxation habits (e.g., mediation, prayer, healing, visualization)

2. Seeking closure of tasks and interpersonal situations—finishing unfinished business

Personal Planning

1. Effective time management day-to-day

2. Life and career planning for the long term

Source: Adams, J. D. (1980). *Understanding and managing stress: A book of readings.* San Diego: University Associates.

Family Life Cycle

Family Life Cycle Stage	Emotional Process of Transition: Key Principles	Second Order Changes in Family Status Required to Proceed Developmentally
1. Between Families: The Unattached Young Adult	Accepting parent/offspring separation	a. Differentiation of self in relation to family of origin b. Development of intimate peer relationships c. Establishment of self in work
2. The Joining of Families Through Marriage: The Newly Married Couple	Commitment to new system	a. Formation of marital system b. Realignment of relationships with extended families and friends to include spouse
3. The Family With Young Children	Accepting new members into the system	a. Adjusting marital system to make space for child or children b. Taking on parenting roles c. Realignment of relationships with extended family to include parenting and grandparenting roles
4. The Family with Adolescents	Increasing flexibility of family boundaries to include children's independence	a. Shifting of parent-child relationships to permit adolescent to move in and out of system b. Refocus on mid-life marital and career issues c. Beginning shift toward concerns for older generation
5. Launching Children and Moving On	Accepting a multitude of exits from and entries into the family system	a. Renegotiation of marital system as a dyad b. Development of adult-to-adult relationships between grown children and their parents c. Realignment of relationship to include in-laws and grandchildren d. Dealing with disabilities and death of parents (grandparents)
6. The Family in Later Life	Accepting the shifting of generational roles	a. Maintaining own and/or couple functioning and interests in face of physiological decline; exploration of new familial and social role options b. Support for a more central role for middle generation c. Making room in the system for the wisdom and experience of the elderly; supporting the older generation without overfunctioning for them d. Dealing with loss of spouse, siblings and other peers and preparation for own death

Source: Carter, E., & McGoldrick, M. (1980). *The family life cycle.* New York: Gardner Press.

Healthy Families

1. Demonstrate a warm and trusting attitude in familial interactions;

2. Are characteristically open and mutually respectful in their interactions and speak honestly and disagree without fear of retribution;

3. Use negotiation rather than power in problem solving;

4. Demonstrate a high level of personal initiative and assume personal responsibility for their individual choices and interests;

5. Promote a definite yet flexible family structure with appropriate distribution of responsibilities and privileges between parents and children;

6. Demonstrate emotional maturity and autonomy;

7. Share common perceptions of reality that are congruent with the social framework of their community;

8. Encourage affective expression for positive and negative emotions; and

9. Demonstrate other signs of well-being such as spontaneity, humor, and recognition of other members' talents.

Source: Lewis, J. M. et al. (1976) in Wilcoxon, S. A. (1985). Healthy family functioning: The other side of family pathology. *Journal of Counseling and Development, 63,* 495–499.

Top Ten Family Stresses

1. Economics/finances/budgeting

2. Children's behavior/discipline/sibling fighting

3. Insufficient couple time

4. Lack of shared responsibility in the family

5. Communicating with children

6. Insufficient "me" time

7. Guilt for not accomplishing more

8. Spousal relationship (communication, friendship, sex)

9. Insufficient family playtime

10. Overscheduled family calendar

Source: Curran, D. (1985). *Stress and the healthy family.* Minneapolis: Winston Press.

Conclusions on Family Stress

1. Husbands and wives vary significantly on what they perceive as top stresses within the same family.

2. Work stresses are allowed to impact the family, but family stresses are not allowed to impact work.

3. Four of the ten most-named stressors in family life have to do with lack of time.

4. Healthy families view stresses as normal, while other families view them as evidence of weakness or failure.

5. Healthy families seek solutions, while stressful families seek blame.

6. Resolving one family stress often gives rise to another equally stressful.

7. The named stress is not always the actual stress.

8. While insufficient money is named as the top stress in most families, the real stress stems from how money is viewed and spent rather than the amount available.

9. Low self-image/self-worth is overwhelmingly a woman's stress.

10. Enjoyable volunteer activity reduces a person's stress level while unenjoyable volunteer activity increases it.

11. The ability to deal effectively with stress is related to how much prior experience the family has had in coping with stress: the more stress experienced the more skills developed.

12. Stress-effective families distinguish between stresses they can and cannot control. They focus their energy on controllable stresses and live with the others.

Source: Curran, D. (1985). *Stress and the healthy family.* Minneapolis: Winston Press.

How to Hold a Family Meeting

A very effective way to bring more harmony and organization into family life is to hold Family Meetings on a weekly basis. There are no rigid rules to follow since you have to do what fits your family the best. But here are some guidelines that will help you get started.

1. Choose a table—any shape, any size—where each member of the family can pull up a chair. Let the toddler join the rest of the group—he'll soon learn not to disrupt. Encourage *every* person who lives in the home to join the meeting. Provide a notebook and pen to make a permanent record of the decisions reached.

2. Have the children take their usual places at the table and keep them for every meeting. Rotate the official duties around the family circle. Carry on this rotation so that everyone in the family who can read and write has a turn. Select a chairperson and a secretary.

3. An agenda may be followed at each meeting. It can be posted during the week and available for all members to write down items they wish to discuss. A possible agenda follows:

   A. Reading of Minutes from previous meeting.
   B. Calendar for the coming week.
   C. Bank and other financial transactions between parents and children.*
   D. Old Business
   E. New Business
   F. Future Plans

   Many families have found it beneficial to follow the reading of the minutes with a discussion of the "nicest things that happened in the week before."

4. Call the very first meeting for the specific purpose of planning family fun to follow. Let each one have a "Say" in what the fun will be. Mother and Dad may offer suggestions but should not force their own ideas. Each individual should have equal opportunity to present ideas and offer alternatives.

Note: The first meetings should last no longer than 15 minutes as this is as long as order can easily be kept in a family not used to acting jointly.

* (*Optional:* You may want to include this as your family gets more experienced in group discussions and decision making).

Suggested Topics:

Family trips
Family Celebrations during holidays
Distribution of family chores
Problems in the home
Celebration of a family member's birthday, election, promotion, etc.
Family projects
Discussion of allowances

Pitfalls to Avoid:

Don't let meetings deteriorate into gripe sessions
This is not a time for parents to sermonize or lecture
Keep the meetings short and to the point
No member should be excluded from the decision-making process
Don't look for negatives—look for positives
Plan meetings at a time and place where *all* family members can attend

Session 8: Developing an Action Plan

The purpose of this session is to help teachers develop a plan of action to implement the activities on fear and stress in their classrooms. The emphasis will be on the three levels of prevention with a focus on infusion of the activities into the daily curriculum.

Overview

This final session will address perhaps the most important part of the training, for it is through the plan of action developed by the teachers that the program will or will not reach success. If the activities are not formally introduced into the curriculum they lose their potential impact. You want to challenge the teachers to expand their skills in observing children and incorporate these methods of addressing some very basic human motivators. Without a sense of security, control and self-worth one cannot become a fully functioning human being. By addressing the predictable fears and stress of children teachers can help them to accomplish these three basic ingredients for success in life.

An activity to help the teachers to stretch their imaginations and expand their own sense of accomplishment follows. It is called "You are More Than You Think" and is adapted from an activity in Jean Houston's book, *The Possible Human* (1981).

Procedures for "You are More Than You Think":
1. Stand up and face the front of the room allowing arms length distance between yourself and others.
2. Extend right arm in front and turn head to the right and locate a point on the wall that is as far as you can see. Do not strain your neck muscles. Then turn head back to center and lower arm.
3. Extend left arm in front and turn head to the left. Then turn head back to center and lower arm.
4. Extend both arms from the side and with head remaining forward swing upper body and arms to the right and then to the left. Return to center and lower arms.
5. Extend right arm in front and turn head to the right picking a new point on the wall and notice how much further this point is than the first point. Do not strain your neck muscles.

Plan of Action

Congratulations for completing this training workshop on children's fear and stress. You should be better equipped to recognize the signs and sources of stress and fear in children and likewise introduce appropriate intervention strategies in your classroom, school, and community. If you have found these sessions to be effective and the materials appropriate for your setting, it will now be important for you to establish a plan of action. Please complete the incomplete statements that follow and then share your responses with another member of the group.

1. I teach grade(s)_____

2. The level of fear or stress in my school and community is

3. The predominant fears and stress in my setting are

4. I will begin to introduce the following strategies in my school or classroom during the year:

    Level 1 Prevention

    Level 2 Prevention

    Level 3 Prevention

5. I have the following resources in my community to handle the children with problems related to fear and stress:

Closing Activities

1. Ask teachers to work in groups of three to design a poster or bumper sticker related to the topic of the workshop. Examples might include:

FEAR IS A FOUR-LETTER WORD

*F*antasy
*E*uphoria
*A*cceptance
*R*eal

2. Have teachers complete a clustering around the words fear or stress. This can be done individually or as a group. Place and circle the word fear on the chalkboard or large newsprint so all can see, then ask individuals to free associate around the word, calling on different people in the group to call out one word at a time, e.g.,

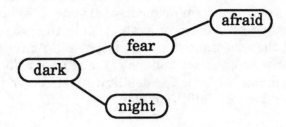

Continue to call on individuals until your board or newsprint is filled with circled words. Then ask each person to construct a paragraph using as many of the words as possible. Ask volunteers to read their paragraphs. This activity again helps them to see the complexity of the issues related to fear and stress and also, since it comes at the end of the workshop, helps them to tie together much of what has been covered. It also enhances collegiality within the group by establishing a common interest. And, finally, the activity can help to solidify a commitment to follow through with the plan of action.

References

Houston, J. (1981). *The possible human.* Boston: Houghton Mifflin.

Session 8
Outline

I.	Purpose of Plan of Action	5 minutes
II.	Activity: You Are More Than You Think	5 minutes
III.	Plan of Action	45 minutes
IV.	Closing Activities	25 minutes
V.	Evaluation	10 minutes

Workshop Evaluation Questionnaire

You will want to conduct a brief evaluation of the training workshops to give yourself feedback on the value of the training to the participants and give the participants an opportunity to reflect upon the experience. A sample evaluation form is included here for your use. You may wish to design your own form or modify this one. The important thing is that you take the time to conduct some form of evaluation of the program. We hope that this Facilitator's Guide and the accompanying Discussion and Activities have been helpful to you and the participants in your workshops. Through your efforts and commitment perhaps fewer children will suffer from the debilitating effects of fear and stress and, better yet, lead more productive and fulfilling lives.

1. As a result of this training: I learned that I _____

    I was surprised that I _____

    I was pleased that I _____

    I was disappointed that I _____

2. The trainer was _____

3. The sessions were: (circle appropriate number)

5	4	3	2	1
Helpful				Not Helpful

4. The supporting activities were:

5	4	3	2	1
Helpful				Not Helpful

Specific Comments:

Appendix 2-A: Fear and Stress Survey

The purpose of this survey is to determine the specific sources of fear and stress in K–8 children and to gather some general information that may help in the development of a teacher's manual, workshop and curriculum guide for children's fears and stress.

I. General Information

Grade level you teach _____

How long have you been in this school? _____

How many years have you taught? _____

II. Sources of Children's Fears and Stress

In a recent study children ages 5–14 identified, among others, the following as sources of their fears and stress:

Dark	Nuclear war	Homework
Monsters	Failure at school	Family Strife
Strangers	Being alone	Change of school
Punishment	Being physically large	Loss
Ghosts	Death	

1. Please list the five sources of fear and stress you think affect the children you teach (you may choose from the above list or add your own).

    a. _____

    b. _____

    c. _____

    d. _____

    e. _____

2. Please list any sources of fear and stress that you think affect the children you teach that are perhaps unique (you do not have to limit your responses to the school setting).

    a. _____

    b. _____

HIAWATHA ELEMENTARY SCHOOL

c. _____

d. _____

e. _____

3. What percent of the children do you feel are negatively affected:

   5–10%, 10–20%, 20–30%, 30–40%, 40–50%, 50–60%, 60–70%, 70–80%, 80–90%, 90+%

4. What percent of the children do you feel are suffering from the debilitating affects of fears or stress:

   5–10%, 10–20%, 20–30%, 30–40%, 40–50%, 50–60%, 60–70%, 70–80%, 80–90%, 90+%

5. What are some of the behaviors or outward signs you have observed that indicate a child is affected by fears or stress, e.g., nail biting, hair twisting, suicide threats?

   a. _____

   b. _____

   c. _____

6. What specific things have your students told you that are fearful distress?

   a. _____

   b. _____

   c. _____

7. Please check all the following statements that apply to you

   a. _____ I would like to know more about how fears and stress can affect children's *learning*.

   b. _____ I would like to know more about how fears and stress can affect children's *mental health*.

   c. _____ I would like to know more about how fears and stress can affect children's *physical health*.

   d. _____ I would like to know more about how children can cope with stress and fear.

   e. _____ I would like to know how to help a child cope with fear and stress.

   f. _____ I would like to have materials and activities I could use in the classroom to help children deal with fear and stress.

Appendix 2-B: Additional Handouts

Techniques for Managing Children During a Crisis*

- Avoid separation of children from parent, if possible.

- Encourage discussion of the incident.

- Encourage creative play re-enacting the crisis.

- Arrange for rumor control.

- Create parent-support group.

- Return to normal routine as soon as possible.

- Build on experience of past crises.

- Consider consultation of health professional if child's behavior continues to cause concern.

* Read "Classroom Activities for Children Exposed to a Violent Event" (Appendix 2-C, page 171) for more information.

Giving Emotional First Aid to Children

1. *Be calm.* Adults' demeanor and bearing will be interpreted by children. Negative or disquieting reactions can cause needless anxiety and panic in children observing them. A measured voice and controlled, patient and relaxed behavior is the goal.

2. *Be honest.* Give supportive information that is truthful. For example, if a child is afraid that his parent has been injured or has forgotten him you can say, "I don't know," or "I'm not sure, but we are trying to find out and we will tell you." Children need to be able to trust the available adults.

3. *Get the child to talk if possible.* Verbal catharsis is helpful in relieving tension, and distraction is useful, especially if the child is injured. Listen carefully.

4. *Inform the child about the plan of action*—even if it is only that "we will wait here until the people who will help us get here." Any structure an adult can provide will be helpful to a child involved in a violent or crisis situation.

5. *Mobilize the child's own resources.* Anything a child can do for himself or another will help him feel more in control. Singing, clapping games, helping younger children with clothing or eating are examples.

6. *Give reassurance and comfort.* Physical contact (hugging, holding hands, a lap) are the basics. Food and drink and a place to snuggle down come next. When possible assure the child of continuing attention.

Questions

1. What are our school's preparations for dealing with crises?

   How much do we know about them?

   Does the school have an emergency plan including a system for communicating with parents?

   What do we need to know about the school's emergency plan?

   What should we do to support and strengthen the school's plan?

2. What crises have we as parents/teachers/administrators experienced with children?

   What were our own reactions and those of other adults?

   What reactions and behaviors were most helpful?

   What reactions and behaviors were least helpful?

   What were some of the reactions and behaviors of the children?

   What can we learn from these experiences?

3. What kinds of crises could occur?

4. What steps should we take to help ourselves and our community manage children more effectively during a crisis? How do we want to follow up on this? List some specific steps we want to take.

Evaluation

1. What were your expectations of the workshop? How were these expectations realized?

2. What segments have been the most useful to you?

3. What segments have been the least useful to you?

4. What changes would you make in the workshop?

Name _____
(Optional)

Appendix 2-C: Classroom Activities for Children Exposed to a Violent Event

Study after study reveals that for children the most stressful aspects of a violent event are:

- Separation from parents or other responsible adults
- Observing over-anxious, hysterical adult reactions to the event

We know that children's reactions will be largely determined by the social and emotional climate provided by those they trust, i.e. parents, teachers and community leaders. Given continued support before, during and in the aftermath of a violent event, most children are able to maintain a sense of security and faith in the people and institutions they know.

In school, emotional coping can be taught to children as well as modeled by adults. The following comments and suggestions are drawn from the many studies of children's reactions to violent events at home and abroad, and from reports of strategies developed by teachers, parents and mental health professionals to help children both anticipate violent events, and actively cope with their emotions after such an event.

The important word here is *active*. Exposure to violence and terror causes a bewildering variety of reactions including high levels of anxiety and aggressive feelings in children, as well as adults. Some adults, faced with uncertainty and threat, may become confused or inefficiently overactive, or else attempt to manage by ignoring the situation.

We know that enforced passivity is highly stressful especially for children. Therefore activity is called for which both addresses the violent or threatening situation and provides an outlet and expression for the internal pressures built up in children as a result.

Children's reactions to disturbing events will of course vary, but their physical proximity and emotional closeness to the event and those involved will in general determine the intensity of response. Children who have already suffered a significant loss, such as death in the family or divorce, and children who have difficulty expressing feelings, may experience particularly powerful reactions, which may or may not be obvious to the observer. The reactions may take place immediately following the event, or appear in the ensuing weeks, months, or years. Conversely, a certain number of children will appear to be unaffected by the event, and this will be normal behavior for them.

The following is an outline of activities addressing, with both teachers and children, the progression of a threat situation followed by a disturbing or violent event.

Part I: *Activities in a Threat Period* lists preparatory activities which will in themselves serve to "innoculate" teachers and students against the stress of uncertainty and possible violence.

Part II: *Classroom Activities Following a Violent Event* would be helpful even if minimal or no preparation had taken place. Unfortunately many violent events are difficult if not impossible to anticipate.

Following a disturbing event, most schools attempt to return to normal routine as soon as possible. Depending on the situation and resources, teachers should allocate some daily time to crisis-related activities. Time spent early on in these activities may serve to reduce the time needed to work through feelings. Children will vary in their interest and in their ability to join such activities. The important thing is to provide children with the opportunity to express themselves or not as they choose.

The rationale for the suggested activities includes the following notions outlined in Community Oriented Preparation for Emergency (COPE) (Ayalon, 1979):

- Stress situations cause distress which must be dealt with if hidden strengths are to be discovered.
- Children of different ages can develop coping patterns suitable to their ages and temperaments.
- Tension relieving activities can integrate emotion, cognition and action in a way that strengthens the child's self image and self confidence.
- Spontaneous and imaginative expression in a variety of media gives children access to supressed worries, which, if alleviated, release additional creative energy.
- Small group discussion in the classroom enables children to know that their emotions are shared by others. It also helps the classroom group feel competent and useful as it addresses and discusses a difficult situation.
- A non-judgmental encouraging atmosphere with emphasis on the creative process will encourage support by the children for each other in difficult times.

In Ayalon's COPE program, stories and poems are used to stimulate discussion of children's personal experiences. Creative writing helps gain self awareness and allows the expression and fulfillment of imaginary wishes. Dramatic play is effective in solving both interpersonal and interpsychic conflicts. Simulation games recreating an event which has happened, or anticipating one which could occur, provide training for complicated situations. Movement, dance and painting, and the fact that teachers ask for and are interested in all these versions of the children's experience of distressing events is reassuring. To them it indicates that adults and children can handle scary events together, and that teachers, as well as adults in general, have confidence in them and value their concerns.

Class discussion and display of all activities and creative productions will both help to identify children needing further assistance and other children who can help provide it.

The combination of activities in the order suggested provides a framework for experiencing and coming to terms with a loss experience. It allows for all of the familiar stages of crisis and grief. In classrooms, as in families, these will be experienced differently by different individuals within a general progression through periods of disbelief, bargaining, anger, depression and acceptance.

Initial *denial/disbelief* that the event has happened is addressed by activities allowing repetition and replay of the event until the reality is absorbed.

Bargaining is implicit in wished-for outcomes and in the various versions played out by the children. These, in turn, allow for expressing *anger* and aggressive feelings in scenarios of blame and getting even.

Depression and sadness find many forms of expression. *Acceptance of reality* is reached in factual discussions when the emotions around the event have been expressed according to the children's needs.

I. Activities in a Threat Period

A. Topics for Discussion by Administrators and Teachers

These discussions should enable staff and teachers to express doubts and reservations, and reduce anxiety while clarifying their personal attitudes towards the activity program.

1. Age-related reactions of children to traumatic events. (See "Techniques for Managing Children During a Crisis," Appendix 2-B, page 167.)
2. Adult fears and communicating to children about fears and other emotions.
3. Teacher provided support for parents handling children's reactions.
4. Information to parents on emergency plan and, if used, post-incident classroom activity plan.
5. Crises likely to occur, choice of incident for simulation drills.
6. Role and task allocation during emergency.
7. Communication/Information system.
    a. Emergency channels
    b. Rumor control
8. First aid, both physical and emotional (see "Giving Emotional First Aid to Children," Appendix 2-B, page 168).
9. Stress management and relaxation techniques for a period of confinement (games, singing, calming exercise, etc.).
10. Preparation for post violent incident classroom activities.

B. Physical Drill of School Emergency Plan in Response to Simulated Violent Event

1. Relocating or removing students to safe area in or out of school buildings.
2. Testing alternative transport home for students.
3. Information to students
    a. Rationale for drill—"We are practicing this so we will know what to do if..."
    b. Rumors and their control—difference between facts, speculation and comment.
    c. Parent-school emergency arrangements.
    d. Student roles during drill, including preparation for possible teacher absence.
    e. Calming Exercise for Children (See Systematic Desensitization Activity, pp. 97–100.)

II. Classroom Activities Following a Violent Event

A. Initial expression of any and all feelings about what happened in discussion.

Example:

Unfinished Sentences:

During the _____ I was scared when _____.
When I heard that _____.
I still think about _____.
When I pass (see, hear) by _____ I think about
_____ and I feel _____.

Drawings to Accompany Sentences:

Pictures of what happened
People it happened to
Yourself (the child) at the time

Composite Picture of Event on Large Board:

Title: "The Event"
Drawing contributions by children

B. Re-enacting the Event

1. Children (or puppets, dolls, etc.) take all roles, including aggressors, victims and rescuers.
2. All versions of the event acceptable including:
   a. Actual occurrences
   b. Wished for outcomes
   c. Scenarios of revenge and retaliation

Point: If much anger is evident, provision of a punching bag (for example) may be appropriate. The children need to know that feelings are acceptable but actions must be limited.

C. Factual Teacher-Lead Discussion

1. Who did what, why
2. What they might have done
3. What we know now that we didn't know then

Point: Cognitive reappraisal of the experience. Children may want to make a model scene of the event accompanying this discussion.

D. Further Activities to Work Through Feelings About the Event

1. Poems
2. Stories
3. Songs—new words to familiar tune
4. Pictures as memorials—"How we will remember..."
5. Letters to those affected by event
6. Visit to event site

Point: If children are anxious or fearful—of the airport, for example—adult support using stress management techniques like relaxation and breathing exercises may be appropriate.

7. Classroom or school assembly visit by expert to answer questions and address safety
8. Safety discussion
9. Updated emergency drill
10. With parents:
    a. Information on school activities related to the crisis.
    b. Support for
       (1) Hearing out children's reactions
       (2) Understanding and managing regressive behavior
       (3) Alert for possible late effects
    c. Support for parents forming their own group to deal with ongoing parental concern and reactions.

References

Ayalon, O. (1979). Community oriented preparation for emergency (COPE). *Death Education, 3,* 223–244.

About ERIC/CASS

Educational Resources Information Center—ERIC

ERIC is a decentralized nationwide information system founded in 1966 and currently sponsored by the Office of Educational Research and Improvement within the U.S. Department of Education. It is the largest education-related database in the world. ERIC is designed to collect educational documents and journal articles and to make them readily available through a number of products and services; e.g., the ERIC database, abstract journals, microfiche collections, online and CD-ROM computer searches, document reproductions, and information analysis publications. The ERIC audience is equally wide-ranging and includes teachers, counselors, administrators, supervisors, policy makers, librarians, media specialists, researchers, students, parents, and other educators and interested persons.

Counseling and Student Services Clearinghouse—CASS

CASS is one of the 16 subject-oriented clearinghouses of the ERIC system. CASS' exceptionally broad coverage includes K–12 counseling and guidance, post-secondary and adult counseling services, and human resource development in business, industry and government. Among the topics addressed are:

- preparation, practice and supervision of counseling professionals
- development of theoretical constructs
- research on programs and practices
- interviewing and testing
- group work
- career planning and development
- employee assistance programs (EAPs)
- training and development
- marriage and family counseling
- student activities
- services to special populations (substance abusers, public offenders, students-at-risk)
- program evaluation

CASS acquires literature in its subject area, processes the information into the ERIC database, and produces a variety of subject-specialized materials. It offers such products as monographs, special issues papers, state-of-the-art studies, computer search analyses, bibliographies and digests. A quarterly newsletter (free upon request) features Clearinghouse activities, products, and articles on timely topics. CASS' professional staff also offers question-answering services, computer searching of the ERIC database, on-site user services with a complete ERIC microfiche collection at the CASS Resources Center and national, state and local workshops on high-priority counseling and human services concerns. We welcome visitors and mail or phone inquiries.

ERIC/CASS
School of Education
University of North Carolina at Greensboro
Greensboro, NC 27412-5001
(800) 414-9769